HIGH
IMPACT
SELLING

Power Strategies
for Successful Selling

HIGH IMPACT SELLING

Power Strategies for Successful Selling

William T. Brooks

GAMEPLAN PRESS

Library of Congress Cataloging-in-Publication Data

Brooks, William T.
    High impact selling.

    Includes index.
    1. Selling.   I. Title.
HF5438.25.B743   1988   658.8'5   87-3567

Editorial/production supervision and
    interior design: *TKM Productions*
Cover design: *Lundgren Graphics, Ltd.*

*This book is dedicated to
the greatest salesperson I have ever known,
the late Clifford W. Brooks.*

*It is also dedicated to
the greatest sales trainer and writer in the world—
the man from whom all of my ideas have sprung,
Ron Willingham.*

Contents

Preface

High Impact Selling offers an exciting new direction in sales training—a direction that is gaining widespread acceptance by many of America's leading corporations.

Both the novice salesperson and the seasoned veteran will find the *high impact selling system* to be practical, simple, and powerfully effective. It will give you the skills and knowledge to sell almost anybody almost anything, almost anywhere. Based on my many years as a sales trainer and consultant, I have explained the system fully and clearly in this challenging book.

This book begins by addressing the need for a new direction in sales training. The constantly changing environment in which selling occurs requires a reevaluation of such current sales training practices as:

1. Regarding product training as the sum and substance of sales training
2. Sales training that is too technique oriented
3. Viewing periodic addresses by motivational speakers as the answer
4. Sales training systems so complicated it takes a genius to learn them

AT LAST: A NEW DIRECTION IN SALES TRAINING

High Impact Selling is based on tested and proven principles and is attuned to the value systems of today's sellers and customers. It encourages you to take charge of your own sales training and to rely on your own efforts to turn selling into an exciting and lucrative career that is worthy of your best efforts. To guide you in your efforts, I have provided an in-depth discussion of three power strategies for selling.

In "Power Strategy #1: Raise Your Customer Impact," we take a close look at why the top 20 percent of all salespeople are responsible for 80 percent of all sales made in this country annually. It also shows how you can develop the kind of impact on customers those highly successful salespeople have and how to use it to boost your sales dramatically.

Chapter 1 defines high customer impact and shows you why it gives you, the salesperson, a competitive edge and how you can increase your customer impact. Chapter 2 goes on to explore the mind set of high impact selling in terms of self-confidence: your belief in yourself, in the selling profession, and in your product. And in Chapter 3 we look at your potential customer's needs and values and how you can utilize the key technique of value-based selling.

In "Power Strategy #2: Master High Impact Selling Skills," we use a simple acronym—IMPACT—to present a powerful six-step system:

Investigate to discover who is interested in your business proposal.

Meet with interested persons to dialog about your proposal.

Probe to find out what potential customers want most and under what conditions they will buy it.

Apply your most appropriate solution to their most compelling needs and desires.

Convince them that they can fulfill their needs and wishes by buying whatever you are selling.

Tie it up and take it home.

Chapters 4 through 9 discuss each of these steps in detail. Thus Chapter 4 introduces you to prospecting and information-gathering techniques to begin your process. Chapter 5 continues with suggestions on an initial meeting with prospects and how to build rapport. Chapter 6, the core of the high impact selling system, shows you how to encourage the process of "listening" people into buying your product. You become the facilitator who enables them to clarify their own wants and needs. Chapter 7—the Apply step—shows you how to convince prospects that your product will meet their needs, and Chapter 8 continues by offering help on how to prompt clients to take positive action by buying your product at your price. The final step— tying up the deal—is discussed in Chapter 9, and Chapter 10 concludes this power strategy by reviewing the high impact system and giving you some practical guidelines for its implementation.

In "Power Strategy #3: How to Master Personal Management Skills," we show you how you can make more money with less effort, and how to fully enjoy everything you do. Special emphasis is given to time management and building enthusiasm.

Specifically, in Chapter 11 we assess how you are using—or wasting—valuable time on the job and how you can regain control of your time in ways that are profitable to you on a daily basis. Chapter 12 offers some thoughts about the valuable entity called enthusiasm and how you can retain it without burnout.

BROAD APPEAL FOR MANY YEARS

The high impact selling system was developed over a period of more than 20 years and has been thoroughly tested and proven. I have been involved in training salespeople for the Chevrolet Division of General Motors, Inc., using similar concepts to those that are explained in this book, and salespeople in some dealerships have boosted their closing average from the typical 17 percent of prospects to a staggering 40 percent closing average.

This book will appeal to a broad range of people—from those who are merely investigating the possibilities of a career in sales, to seasoned salespeople in all selling categories and types of selling situations.

Introduction

You can boost your success in selling by using the three power strategies presented in this book:

1. Raise your impact on customers
2. Master high impact selling skills, and
3. Improve your personal management skills

Whether you are a novice salesperson or a seasoned veteran, you'll find the "Brooks method" to be highly practical, simple to follow, and powerfully effective.

NEEDED: A NEW DIRECTION IN SALES TRAINING

Most of the sales training available today has lost touch with the constantly changing environment in which selling takes place. This is not a criticism of any of my colleagues in sales training or the many corporations that invest millions each year in teaching people to sell. It is merely a statement of the major fallacies that are apparent in most of the approaches used during the last two decades.

You've probably experienced the frustrations of one (or all) of the following fallacies of most of the current sales training systems:

1. *Most corporations regard product training as sales training.* The idea seems to be that the only thing people need to make them successful at selling is to learn the features of their products or services. As we shall see, product training is vital, but it is not the whole picture. Any company that merely calls its sales force in to acquaint its people with new products is sending them out with only one weapon to fight a multi-faceted war.

2. *Many sales training approaches are technique oriented.* They bombard salespeople with myriads of techniques designed to equip them to regard the customer as an adversary, or perhaps an idiot, and close in for the "kill." In case you haven't noticed, today's customer is an entirely different creature from those of even a decade ago.

3. *Bringing in a motivational speaker periodically to get salespeople all "hyped up" is another typical approach to sales training.* But overdosing on motivation produces the long-term effect of sales burnout—it creates the same impact as keeping a car's motor revved up constantly without ever putting it into gear. Motivation without a plan only generates frustration.

4. *A major fallacy of current sales training is that it is based on such complicated systems it takes a genius to learn them.* Many of the current systems are based on clever buzzwords that have little meaning to the typical person, complex ideas that are used to turn salespeople into amateur psychologists or sly manipulators, and closing techniques designed to trap prospects into saying "yes." Even if salespeople are able to learn such systems, they often find them in conflict with their own values.

AT LAST: A NEW DIRECTION IN SALES TRAINING

Keeping pace with the ever-changing value systems of the marketplace calls for a highly adaptable approach to selling.

High impact selling represents a new and exciting direction in sales training—a direction that is gaining widespread acceptance by many of America's leading corporations.

It is based on tested and proven principles and attuned to the new value systems of today's sellers and customers.

You'll find the high impact selling system

- So simple to learn and easy to implement that anyone can do it
- Founded on basic principles of human relations so you'll know the *why* behind every *how*
- Integrity-based so you'll never have to violate your own values
- Filled with extremely practical ideas you can begin to use immediately
- Adaptable to any product, service, or selling situation
- Dynamic enough to meet the challenges of selling in the ever-changing environment of the eighties and nineties

TAKING CHARGE OF YOUR OWN SALES TRAINING

A recent study by Columbia University revealed that the typical salesperson showed a great reluctance to make sales calls. For example, the average sales call is made after 11:00 AM every day, and the typical salesperson spends less than 90 minutes a day in actual customer contact.

Perhaps you too hate making sales calls and put them off as long as you can each day. You may even have played with the idea that selling is just not for you. If so, you have a lot of company. Studies show that one-third of all salespeople, at any given time, are actively looking for jobs that require no selling. If that's where you are coming from, let me urge you to read this entire book and give high impact selling a solid try before you throw in the towel.

One of the great myths of selling is that some people are "born salespeople." I have a friend who has been an obstetrician for many years. "I've delivered thousands of babies over the years," he says, "but I've never delivered a salesperson."

When you were a little kid, your parents always told you what to do. Later in life, other adults planned your days and activities for you.

However, when you became an adult, you discovered that you had the right and the responsibility to make your own choices, to plan your own education, and to control your own actions.

If you are like many of the thousands of salespeople I've trained, you've been looking to someone else to make all your decisions and to plan your sales training for you. "After all," you might have reasoned, "my sales manager is my boss, and he or she knows a lot more about it than I do . . . . Anyway, it's only a job. Besides, if I do what others tell me to do, then I can always blame anything that goes wrong on them."

Certainly you have to listen to your boss, and many bosses are eager to share information that can help you become successful at selling. Yet, in all the years I've been working with sales managers, I've never met one who did not encourage his or her salespeople to learn all they could from any reliable source, and I've never met a salesperson who has been fired for taking responsibility for his or her own sales training.

If you regard selling as nothing more than a job that pays the rent, you're in for some exciting discoveries in this book. I'm going to show you how you can take charge of your own sales training and turn selling into an exciting and lucrative career that is worthy of your best efforts.

A BRIEF OVERVIEW

Selling is a science, based on documented principles that can be learned by anyone of average intelligence. As a science, it has an underlying view of human nature, and a concomitant set of principles is learned by both study and experimentation, and has very useful applications to daily life.

Like any science, it is constantly changing to challenge old assumptions, to embrace new discoveries, and to adapt to new situations. What you'll find in *High Impact Selling* is a blending of the best of the tested and proven techniques and challenging new concepts that are working well for thousands of salespeople in the new selling environment.

To make it simple for you, the book is divided into three sections, each examining in detail one *power strategy for selling:*

Power Strategy # 1:
Raise Your Customer Impact

This section takes a close look at why the top 20 percent of all salespeople are responsible for 80 percent of all sales made in this country annually. You'll learn how you can have the kind of impact on customers those highly successful salespeople have and how to use it to boost your sales dramatically.

Power Strategy # 2:
Master High Impact Selling Skills

Here we introduce you to a powerful six-step system that covers every aspect of selling—from prospecting to closing sales. The system is so simple you can learn it with minimal effort and time; it is so complete you will always know exactly what to do next; and it is so powerful you will wonder why you ever tried anything else.

Power Strategy # 3:
How to Master Personal Management Skills

The last section of the book focuses on how professional salespersons manage their careers by managing their entire lives. You'll learn how to make more money with less effort, and how to fully enjoy everything you do.

In all, high impact selling is the most effective, most potent, and most productive selling system every devised. It was developed over a period of more than 20 years and has been thoroughly tested and proven. Using the simple techniques we present in the following chapters, many Chevrolet dealers across America have boosted their closing average from the typical 17 percent of prospects to a staggering 40 percent closing average.

If you're as excited as I am about what high impact selling can do for you, begin your first reading of "Power Strategy # 1."

Raise Your Customer Impact

PURPOSE

The purpose of this first section of the book is

1. To discover what customer impact is and why it determines success or failure in selling
2. To learn how to develop greater customer impact
3. To uncover the greatest secret of impact selling

HIGH IMPACT SELLING

Have you ever noticed that some salespeople seem to work shorter hours, enjoy their work more, yet make more sales (and money) than others of equal ability and training—regardless of what they are selling?

What's the difference?

The logical answer is that some salespeople are more effective than others. But what does it mean to be effective?

My dictionary gives three definitions of *effective* which help to get at the answer:

1. Strikingly impressive
2. Ready for service or action
3. Capable of producing a desired outcome

When you combine those three concepts, you get what I call the high impact salesperson.

> The High Impact Salesperson:
> A strikingly impressive person, ready
> for service or action, and capable of
> producing maximum sales with
> minimal time and effort.

In down-to-earth words, high impact selling is knowing how to get the attention of the right people, what to do with it while you've got it, and how to turn what you know into what you can spend.

Three Dimensions of High Impact Selling

High impact salespeople are effective in three vital areas of selling:

First, they have a powerful impact on the customer, which enables them to find more qualified prospects and influence more of them to buy.

Second, they have mastered high impact selling skills that enable them to boost their closing average and make maximum use of their prime selling time.

Third, they have developed personal management techniques that enable them to increase their prime selling time.

In this section, we will explore the first of these three areas. Although we will make frequent references to the others, we will save detailed treatment until later.

CHAPTER 1

In Search of
High Customer Impact

PURPOSE

High customer impact is the ability to convince prospects that what you have to say is important, that what you claim is true, and that it is to their benefit to act on your recommendations. In this chapter, you'll discover:

1. What high customer impact is
2. Why it gives you the competitive edge
3. How to get more of it

> *"The heart has its reasons,*
> *which reason does not know."*
> *—Blaise Pascal*

WHAT MAKES A WINNER?

Why is it that more than 60 percent of all the sales made in America each year are made by the top 5 percent of all salespeople?

If you ask 100 salespeople that question, you'll probably get 100 different answers.

"They've got products that are in great demand," some will say.

"They've got good territories," others will answer.

"They just work harder," another will confess.

Studies show that most salespeople in the top 5 percent would do well selling almost anything, almost anywhere, and that they often work fewer hours than most of the salespeople in the bottom 20 percent.

No, the answer to why the top 5 percent of all salespeople have become the real champions in selling is simply this: *they have and use high customer impact.* They have and use the power to influence many people to buy.

In this chapter, let's search out what high customer impact is, how it can give you the winner's edge, and how to get it.

I. WHAT IS CUSTOMER IMPACT?

One of the best ways to understand customer impact is to put yourself in the customer's shoes.

Your doorbell rings, you answer it and discover it's a salesperson who wants to come in and show you a miraculous new can opener that can be yours for a phenomenally low price. You're courteous, but you quickly get rid of that salesperson. If he or she gets pushy, you might even speak abruptly and slam the door.

However, later that evening an insurance salesperson keeps an appointment with you, and you spend more than an hour soaking up every word he or she says. The upshot is that you obligate yourself to spend hundreds of times what you would have spent on the can opener.

What's the difference? Why is it that we will listen intently to everything one person says, while we won't give another the time of day?

The obvious answer is that you were more interested in insurance than you were in a can opener. But that's only a surface answer, and it raises an even more important question: How did the insurance salesperson awaken your interest and convince you that it was to your advantage to spend time listening to what he or she had to say?

Here are four principles that make the answer crystal clear:

> Customer Impact Principle # 1:
> We pay attention to people we believe
> have something important to tell us.

That's the beginning of high customer impact. It's your capacity to convince people that what you have to say is important to them.

Again, put yourself in that customer's shoes. All day long, people are trying to gain your attention. The boss wants you to hear or read instructions; family members want you to do things for them; friends and neighbors have ideas they want to tell you; television, newspapers, and radio bombard you with appeals to buy things, and on and on. According to communications experts, the typical person receives about 1,800 messages a day that suggest some form of action.

What happens to us is that we learn to tune out the unwanted messages; we learn to filter out all but those messages we think are important to us. Thus, high customer impact is the capacity to break through all those thousands of messages and convince a prospect that what you have to say really matters to him or her.

How can you do that? Although the process involves many steps, principle # 2 provides a telling clue.

> Customer Impact Principle # 2:
> People buy for their own reasons;
> not for yours or mine.

Champion salespeople know that prospects typically could not care less if they win a trip to Hawaii, or a new car, or even a yacht.

Every prospect you call on has his or her own needs, interests, and desires. It's as if we all have an inner radio that is pretuned to pick up only one station—WII-FM. That stands for What's In It For Me?

During training experiences with thousands of salespeople, I have observed that the greatest single mistake they consistently make is that they fail to broadcast their messages over their prospects' station, WII-FM. Their focus is on why *they* want to sell, instead of *who would want to buy what they're selling*, and why their prospects would want to buy.

One good example of how this "blindspot" shows up in most salespeople's attitudes is our preoccupation with handling objections. We read, study, and practice 8,000 ways to "overcome objections," rather than searching out how to connect with what the customer wants and how to supply it.

The real champions in selling see their task as helping people get what they want. If you could really grasp that one insight, it alone would make this entire book worth many times what you paid for it and all the time you'll invest in reading it. In fact, as you go along, I hope you'll notice that we keep bringing everything back to that vital principle: Nothing can give you as much customer impact as knowing how to make your every appeal to the prospect's self-interests.

That leads us to the next vital insight into what gives a salesperson high customer impact.

Customer Impact Principle # 3:
People do not want to be sold;
they want to buy.

Have you ever noticed that when a friend or acquaintance shows you a product he or she is happy with the most common expression is, "I bought it from . . ."? It's only when we are unhappy with a purchase we've made that we say, "He *sold* it to me!"

The reason is simple. We Americans are an independent bunch; we want to make up our own minds about the things we do and buy. We resent it when we feel coerced, manipulated, or tricked into doing or buying anything.

What happens when a product or service is sold? The most direct answer is that someone makes a decision to buy. We will listen to (even appreciate) information about a product, service, or company; we will ask questions about things we don't understand; and we will even receive some gentle persuasion to help us make up our minds. But the moment we feel someone is trying to manipulate, intimidate, or dominate, we raise our defenses and prepare to put up a good fight.

The real champions in the sales game know that when a salesperson and a customer get locked into a war of the wills, the salesperson always loses. Their emphasis is on assisting people in making the decision to buy, instead of on selling.

Customer Impact Principle # 4:
Buying is basically an emotional response.

The two most basic reasons any of us buy anything are fear of loss and desire for gain. We buy because we want to avoid some loss we are either experiencing or expect may occur, or we buy because we hope to gain something from the purchase.

If you question that, consider your most recent major purchase. You may have gathered a lot of information about it because you wanted to buy wisely; you may have shopped around because you wanted to get the best value for your money; you may even have thought about it a great deal because you wanted to make sure it was right for you. Ultimately, however, I would bet my bottom dollar that you decision to buy or not buy was sparked by a fear of something you hoped to avoid or a desire for something you hoped to gain.

What I'm basically saying is that buying is primarily an emotional response. It may be tempered by logic, it may be guided by common sense and reason, and it may be delayed by conflicting interests. But what causes us to sign on the dotted line is emotion.

As we shall see more fully later, that suggests several important aspects of customer impact:

First, it suggests that people buy benefits for themselves—not features, products, services, or even corporate reputations.

Second, it suggests that a strong empathy for the customer is absolutely vital for success in selling.

Third, it means that being the sort of salesperson people enjoy doing business with is an extremely valuable asset.

If you want to see your customer impact rise sharply, put your heart into your work. Learn how to connect with your customers' feelings and how to help them find and fulfill their desires or overcome their fears.

Cavett Robert, the great sales trainer, says it this way: "You tell from the head, you sell from the heart!"

So, What Is High Customer Impact?

High customer impact is the ability to gain and hold the attention of the right people and to influence them to buy. It's your capacity to get people to tune out the distractions and listen to you, and eventually to follow your lead in a buying decision.

Believe me, if you can do that, you can make more money, have more control over your life, and gain greater recognition in selling than in almost any profession available to you.

I would suggest that high customer impact is what, more than any other single factor, separates the winners from the losers in the selling profession.

II. CUSTOMER IMPACT: THE WINNER'S EDGE

A few years ago, a racehorse named Achmed became one of the first horses in history to win more than $1 million in a single season. During that same season, there was another horse that came in second in almost every race Achmed won.

Interestingly, Achmed won 15 times as much money as the horse that consistently came in second. Later, the champion was sold for ten times more money than the second runner.

Does that mean that Achmed was 15 times faster than his nearest competitor? That question intrigued a sportswriter, so he made a study of the times logged by the two horses. Achmed's finishing times averaged only 3 percent faster than the slower horse.

Simply stated, the champion that year had a winner's edge of only 3 percent over his nearest competitor, but it was enough to bring his owner 15 times more prize money and give him ten times as much value.

When it comes to making a sale, there are only winners and losers—no one comes in second. You either make the sale or you don't, and the winner gets 100 percent of the money.

For most salespeople, income is directly proportional to the number of sales made. Although you may be able to change jobs often enough to remain ahead of a draw, or you may jump from one salaried selling job to another and keep some income coming in, sooner or later, it will catch up with you. *If you don't close sales, you won't make a living as a salesperson.*

Don't Just Show Up for the Game;
Play to Win

This book is clearly not about "just making a living"—that's the loser's mentality. Losers feel privileged merely to be in a big game, but winners always play to win it.

As a successful college football coach for 14 years, I learned that you can almost always predict the outcome of a championship game by listening to what the coaches and players of the two teams say before the starting gun sounds.

The 1986 Super Bowl offers a good example of how it works. The Chicago Bears won it decisively.

Make no mistake about it: the New England Patriots brought a great team to the championship game. They had many talented players and excellent coaching, and they had overcome great adversity and beat out some strong teams on their road to the biggest game of the year in the National Football League.

But the difference in the two teams showed clearly throughout the whole season. The Patriots seemed surprised that they had made the playoffs, shocked that they'd won their conference championship, and amazed that they'd earned a right to play in the Super Bowl.

"We're just glad to be here and have an opportunity to play in this game," several of their players told the press in the week before the big game.

However, the Bears had decided before the season started that it was to be their year to win it all. They were convinced they could win every game they played that year, and they did win all but one.

"No team in football can beat us!" boasted their cocky quarterback Jim McMahon before the big game. Then he and the Bears confidently went onto the field and backed up their claim with a dazzling performance. When it was all over, they were clearly the champs.

III. CUSTOMER IMPACT: HOW TO GET MORE OF IT

I suspect that you want to become a winner at the selling game or you wouldn't be reading this book. In fact, you may already be a winner. Losers seldom read books like this, but winners read anything and everything that can help them keep their winner's edge honed to razor sharpness.

So far, we've seen that the ability to gain and hold the attention of enough of the right people is what gives the top 5 percent of salespeople their winning edge.

If you have a champion's heart, your next question is likely to be, "How can I get more customer impact?"

In a way, that's what this whole book is about. Every idea in this book is designed to do one thing: to enable you to connect with and influence enough of the right people to do the right things to get whatever you want out of life. Let's take a brief look now at how to boost your customer impact.

I've been around selling all my life. My father sold for 43 years, and I've been selling all my adult life. Even when I was coaching, most of what I was doing was selling. What's more, I've had some excellent teachers and mentors in the selling profession. More recently, I've spent many years training salespeople for some of America's leading corporations.

During all that time, I've noticed that the salespeople who have high customer impact reflect three basic qualities:

1. Strong personal attributes and attitudes
2. Specialized knowledge and skills
3. A propensity for doing the right things at the right times

What we are talking about is people with positive attitudes, in real situations, dealing with real motivational forces, and taking tangible actions to produce desired results.

Focus on Relationships

The bottom line is that successful selling depends upon building and maintaining the right kinds of relationships with prospective customers.

It includes being liked, but it is by no means limited to that. There's no place in the winner's circle for salespeople who can't get along well with others, yet I've met many salespeople who were thoroughly likeable but couldn't sell ice water in a desert.

The ancient Greeks gave us a word that gets at the nature of what I'm talking about. The word is *symbiosis* and it means "living together in a mutually beneficial relationship"—a relationship that provides enough benefits for all of the partners to view it as valuable. It's what someone called a "win–win situation," and for salespeople it means always making sure that customers get enough value to more than justify what they invest.

To reiterate, if you want to increase your customer impact, you'll have to focus on three essential areas:

1. *What kind of person you are.* Impact grows out of the way you feel about yourself, about others, and about what you are doing.

To get a feeling about the level of your customer impact, we'll need to look at the question, What is there about me that would make people want to buy from me?

2. *What you know.* Your most valuable selling tool is not your mouth—as most salespeople seem to believe—but your mind.

High customer impact grows out of what you know about people, about selling, and about what you are selling. It also has to do with how you apply what you know to getting people to do what *you* want them to do.

3. *What you do.* Of course, nothing works unless you do. But there's more to it than that. Some of the hardest working salespeople in the world are also some of the least successful. High impact selling involves doing the right things, at the right time, and in the right way to obtain the desired response.

TO SUM IT ALL UP . . .

The key to success in selling is to have high customer impact—to be able to influence enough of the right people to do the right thing, at the right time, to get whatever you want out of life.

That can only happen when you put yourself in the prospective customer's shoes and understand that

1. People only pay attention to those they believe have something important to say to them.
2. People buy for their reasons, not for yours or mine.
3. People don't want to be sold—they want to buy.
4. Buying is basically an emotional response.

The best way to boost your customer impact is to cultivate an empathy for the customer and to understand his or her needs, interests, and desires.

ACTION STEPS

Here are some questions to help you think about what you just read:

1. What is there about you and your presentation that makes people believe that what you have to say is important to them?

2. What do you do to appeal to your customer's interests and desires?

3. Do you see your primary activity basically as selling or as helping people make buying decisions?

4. What will you do differently after having read this chapter?

CHAPTER 2

The High Impact Selling Mind Set: A New Science of Self-Motivation

PURPOSE

The purpose of this chapter is to explore how high credibility affords you high customer impact and how to boost your credibility through

1. Belief in the selling profession
2. Belief in yourself
3. Belief in what you are selling
4. High personal integrity

> *If you ain't sold,*
> *you can't sell!*

HIGH IMPACT SELLING CALLS FOR A NEW MIND SET

There has been a tremendous shift in the value system of our society during the last two decades, and the new values call for a totally different approach to selling.

When I first entered the direct sales business many years ago, I was told that the way to sell was through manipulation, intimidation, and domination. I was instructed that the best way to get appointments was essentially to lie about the purpose of my call, that the best way to make add-on sales was to switch contracts on my customers, and that selling was totally a numbers game in which you'd hit an area quickly, talk fast, and set people up for the kill. The "golden rule" was bent to say, "Do unto others, then split!" Such underhanded tactics nauseated me then and turn me off now more than ever.

Unfortunately that once popular approach to selling is still espoused by some sales trainers and companies. It hasn't been all that long since one of the most popular books on selling was entitled *Selling Through Intimidation*. High-pressure tactics, tricky closes, and speed-talking still lurk behind a surprising number of sales training systems.

The fact is that most conventional sales training programs have not kept pace with the shifting value systems of our society. Too much of the emphasis is still on clever closing techniques, overselling strategies, and tricky question methods that are used to trap customers into buying things they really don't want. Then, too, the great majority of schemes used to motivate salespeople have centered on artificial gimmicks, fanatical hoopla, and superficial recognition.

An Emerging New Science of Selling and Self-Motivation

But take heart! A whole new science of selling is emerging and, with it, a totally different approach to motivating people both to sell and to buy.

More and more companies are awakening to the reality that dealing with today's consumers and professional buyers is a brand new ballgame. They are discovering that the typical prospect is better educated, more discriminating, and much more value conscious than his or her counterpart of a few decades ago.

In response to this challenge, sales trainers and writers are beginning to find an ever-broadening acceptance for a values-based approach to sales training and motivation. More and more people are coming to recognize that personal and professional credibility is the most vital ingredient for success in selling.

Success in selling does not come from making single sales, or from tricking customers into buying. It comes from building repeat business, from referrals, and from cultivating a reputation as an honest person.

Everything I have ever experienced in buying, selling, and training others to sell has convinced me of the following principle:

> Credibility Principle # 1:
> They've gotta' believe you
> before they'll buy from you!

Dale Carnegie, who trained literally thousands of salespeople, business leaders, and public speakers in ways to win friends and influence people, would often stop his trainees and shout: "I don't believe you! I don't think anyone else will believe you! If you believe what you are saying, make us believe it!"

HOW TO MAKE PEOPLE BELIEVE YOU

Ralph Waldo Emerson may have been right in his day when he said: "If a man ... make a better mouse-trap than his neighbor, tho' he build his house in the woods, the world will make a beaten path to his door."

However, any salesperson who faces the daily realities of a highly competitive marketplace knows that the era of the "beaten path" is gone forever. You not only have to have a better mousetrap; you have to convince every person you call upon that it's better, that you and your company are reliable, and that what you are offering is worth more to them than the money it will cost them. As any salesperson who has made more than half a dozen calls will tell you, that's a big assignment.

What's more, many potential customers have become jaded by outlandish claims from unethical operators. Too many empty promises have made them cynical about everything they hear, and frequent high-pressure tactics from salespeople have forced them to develop formidable resistance to everything you say and do.

Selling may look like "a piece of cake" to the outsider or novice. The idea of dressing up in nice clothes, driving around in your car as you please all day, and making big money may look like a "dream life" to someone who has never tried it. But anybody who has been out there pitching against all the competition and cynicism knows that making people believe you can be a real challenge.

So, how can you break through all of that and make cynical prospects become believing customers? That brings us to principle number two:

> Credibility Principle # 2:
> You can only convince others
> of what you believe!

Probably the greatest enemy you face in making a sale is the tension that exists in the selling situation. Unless you can turn that tension into trust, you will never be able to break through all the resistance and close the sale.

Behavioral psychologists have defined what they call the "territorial imperative." By studying the lower animals, they discovered that virtually every living creature—including humans—marks out an area that he or she will defend to the death against any intruder. When that space is invaded, the animal examines the intruder very closely to determine if it is "friend" or "foe." Only when the animal feels that the invader will do them no harm does he or she relax.

That is a very helpful insight to keep in mind when you telephone or call upon a new prospect. It suggests that the way you look, everything you say and do, and even your attitudes are important. In later chapters, we'll look at how you can break through the tension and build a strong trust bond. Right now, let's focus on where it begins.

CREDIBILITY FOUNDATION # 1:
YOUR BELIEF IN SELLING AS A
WORTHY PROFESSION

Have you ever noticed what happens when you ask most salespeople what they do for a living? You'll get answers like:

"I'm in real estate."

"I work for ... "

"I'm a customer consultant."

Why is it that most salespeople hedge so much about their profession? Why not say:

"I sell homes," or "I sell investment property."

"I sell cars for ... "

"I'm a salesperson."

I think there are two parts to the answer.

1. *The first part of it may be that they don't want to cause people to start building up a wall of resistance to them.* After all, the typical person has a pretty low opinion of salespeople in general.

Ask a hundred people what word immediately comes to their minds when they hear the term *salesperson*, and they'll respond with pest, bull, pushy, boring, pressure, money-grabber, sneaky, and crooked.

Many of them have been exposed to some pretty manipulative, perhaps even unethical, practices by salespeople. For example, you've probably heard the "angel close" routine many insurance salespeople have used. That's where the salesperson asks a prospect and his wife to play out a scenario that goes something like this:

"Charlie, let's imagine that you have died... you're an angel looking down on the world, and you see Mary sitting alone on the sofa comforting your two small children. ... You notice she's crying, Charlie, because there's no money to pay for your home, to feed the children, to pay for their education. ... Suddenly the doorbell rings and a mailman hands her an envelope, from our insurance company. She breaks into a big smile when she sees that it has a check in it, but suddenly she bursts into tears because she notices that the check has no signature. ... It is not signed because you did not sign it Charlie. ... You have an opportunity right now, Charlie—SIGN THAT CHECK!"

Almost every business has its classics in high-pressure tactics: the "turkey-plucking" negotiations between a car salesperson and a sales manager, the "give your child a fighting chance" pitch of book and computer companies, and the "bait and switch" techniques used by so many direct sales organizations.

I have some good news for you! You don't have to answer for every unethical peddler, drummer, and con artist who ever be-smirched the profession of selling! Certainly you have to recognize and deal with the fact that most people have a natural resistance to unethical salespeople. It won't take you long to overcome it, however, if you are open and forthright in your dealings with your customers.

To be sure, you have to demonstrate that you are honest and trustworthy, but the best way to begin that is be proud of your profession as a salesperson.

2. *Many salespeople are ashamed of their profession because they feel it has no prestige.*

There may have been a time when many people went into sales because they couldn't do anything else—thus, the old stereotype of an occupation that requires minimal intelligence and education, few skills, and little more than a "gift of gab."

In case you haven't noticed, that image has been outdated; by any method of keeping score, today's successful salesperson is a true professional—in every sense of that word.

Let's take a quick look at some common vocational standards and see how the selling profession measures up.

Money.   Studies show that top salespeople are among the highest paid professionals in America. It is not unusual to find salespeople who make more money than the chief executive officers of the corporations they work for, and many salespeople actually turn down management positions because taking them would mean a cut in pay.

Prestige.   Salespeople are increasingly showing up on the boards of community organizations, as civic leaders, and in other positions usually reserved for only the "top dogs" in a community.

Specialized skills and training.   Selling in today's complex world of commerce and trade often requires as much specialized knowledge and skill as many of the "old line" professions such as medicine, law, and banking.

Value to clients.   Just as other professionals render services their clients are willing to pay for, salespeople enjoy a unique relationship with their clientele. Most people in our society have learned to look to qualified salespeople for information, guidance, and reassurance in virtually all their buying decisions.

Simply stated, selling is an honorable profession that is worthy of your best efforts. I would even go further and say that you owe it to yourself, to your company, to your clients, and to your colleagues to either accept and foster a positive attitude toward selling or move on to another occupation.

That sets the stage for the next crucial foundation for building trust and making people believe you.

CREDIBILITY FOUNDATION # 2:
YOUR BELIEF IN YOURSELF

Communications experts tell us that more than 80 percent of the signals we send to others are communicated nonverbally—through our eyes, our facial expressions, our gestures, our appearance, our attitudes, and so on. That means that for every statement you make, you send at least four nonverbal signals to your prospect.

Typically, people are nine times more likely to pick up the way you feel about your own credibility from visual signals than from what you say. That suggests the next credibility principle:

> Credibility Principle # 3:
> The more you believe in yourself,
> the easier it is to get others
> to believe what you say.

A strong, positive self-concept is probably the most valuable personal attribute any salesperson can have.

More than any other single factor (perhaps more than all other factors combined), the way you see yourself determines the way you see and are seen by others, and it shapes everything you say and do. It shows up in the way you dress, walk, talk, sit, laugh, and what you do with your eyes and hands—all the things people watch while they are deciding whether or not to believe you.

Yet many of the salespeople who show up at my seminars have very low self-esteem and almost no self-confidence. You can spot it by their reluctance to look you in the eyes, their unkempt appearance, their timid voices, and their ill-at-ease gestures. Sometimes, though, low self-esteem is reflected in a person's flamboyance, loud voice and boisterous laughter, and transparent ego. Of course, those are the very symptoms people look for when they are sizing up the credibility of what you say.

I don't want to play amateur psychologist and tell you whether or why you have such low self-esteem, and I don't have space here to tell you how you can build a solid self-image. However, I do want to highlight two hazards of the selling profession that often create tremendous self-image problems.

1. *Cognitive dissonance:* Don't let that term scare you. It's a psychologist's way of saying that you feel you are called upon to act in a way that is inconsistent with the way you see yourself.

For example, maybe you've been trained to treat prospects in ways you feel are manipulative, abusive, or even unethical. Or, to keep your job, you may be required to stretch the truth, hide certain facts, or cover up for poor quality or service. As a result, you may even find yourself lying to prospects because you think it will help you close a sale. All of this poses a problem because you see yourself as an honest person who respects other people, and that's quite different from the way you feel compelled to act.

I don't want to give you a lot of advice about how to solve the dilemma. I always say in my seminars that Socrates gave a lot of advice, and they killed him.

Let me simply share with you how I've handled it. I decided a long time ago that I would not work for anybody who required me to violate my personal value system to sell their products or services. My own peace of mind and my credibility with my clients means too much for me to destroy them over a few bucks I might make through high-pressure tactics or unethical practices.

Besides, I learned very early in the selling game that if I could not believe in the people I was working for, I surely couldn't convince anyone else to do business with them. Of course, this does not mean you and your company have to live up to all the expectations of every customer you serve. Some people simply cannot be satisfied, and others consider anything that has to do with selling to be manipulative. What it does mean is that you have to operate in a way consistent with your own self-image to have any hope of making others believe in you.

2. *Fear of rejection:* Get enough doors slammed in your face and you can begin to feel pretty rotten about yourself.

Let's face it, regularly being told "no" is a normal part of the selling game. In fact, if everyone you pitch to says "yes," chances are pretty good you are not talking to enough people.

Fear of rejection can cause you to develop a great reluctance about making sales calls; it can also make you timid about asking for an order and can keep you so depressed that you waste your most valuable selling time worrying about personal matters. There are two keys to overcoming fear of rejection:

First, recognize that rejection of a business proposal does not mean personal rejection.

In Chapter 1, we saw that people buy for their reasons, not yours or mine. The opposite is also true: People refuse to buy for their own reasons. They may like you, respect you, and generally feel very positive about all their dealings with you, but they may refuse your business proposal for their own personal reasons. It takes some work to move from intellectually accepting this idea to incorporating it into your emotional value system.

The second and most powerful way to overcome fear of rejection is to believe so strongly in what you are doing that you will not be denied.

A major part of our identity as human beings comes from our usefulness—from our performance of worthwhile work. It is one of the most vital ways we express our uniqueness, our individuality, our personality. Thus, a big part of believing in yourself is believing in what you do all day.

Each year, I travel all over the country conducting from 150 to 200 seminars, giving speeches, and consulting with businesses. It's an exhausting schedule, but I love it. Why? It's because I believe so strongly in what I'm doing that I can't think of anything I'd rather be doing.

When people reject my business proposals I just move on to the next prospect, knowing that what I have to offer is worthwhile. You owe it to yourself, your clients, and everyone in your life to believe so strongly in what you are doing that you will not be denied.

The more I sell, the more I am sure that enthusiasm is not the "hyped-up hoopla" that comes from noisy meetings and slogans.

Enthusiasm is believing that something is worthy of your best efforts, and believing that you can do it.

When You Believe, You Can Make Others Believe

My biggest claim to fame is that I followed Vince Lombardi as head coach. No, I never coached the Green Bay Packers. In 1974, I accepted the position of coach at a college that had not had a football team in 25 years. The last coach they had had was Vince Lombardi.

As you can imagine, resurrecting a football program that had been dead for a quarter of a century was quite a challenge. We lined up a bunch of freshmen for our first game and did surprisingly well against a strong team. During our first year, we won five games and lost four.

In each of the games we lost, we were leading at halftime and could have won, but our players would sit around during halftime and talk about how they could not believe they were winning. They had been reading the newspapers. They'd go back onto the field and fall apart.

However, in the tradition of Lombardi, we kept hammering away at the importance of believing in yourself. During my eight years of coaching there, we only had one losing season.

After winning a big game against a highly successful school, the opposing coach came into our locker room to congratulate us. "You know, you really don't have great players," he told me privately, "but your players think they are better than they really are."

"Coach," I responded, "that's what makes them great players! They believe in themselves!"

I think the legendary Lombardi would have been proud of his former school that day.

CREDIBILITY FOUNDATION # 3:
YOUR BELIEF IN WHAT YOU ARE SELLING

A third way to establish credibility with your customers is to believe firmly in what you are selling. That leads us to another important principle of credibility:

Credibility Principle # 4:
Your customer will never believe in
the value of your product or service
any more strongly than you do!

When you walk into a prospect's home or office, you may be the only person on the premises who believes in the value of your product or service. However, your confidence in what you are selling can often make prospects just as enthusiastic that it is right for them.

According to the old school of sales training, belief in your product or service meant you had to convey the idea that it was the greatest one of its kind in the world. That approach made selling very hard for truly honest salespeople, and it strained their credibility with rational people.

Chevrolet is one of my largest clients, and I've had the privilege of working with many of their dealers and salespeople. It would be foolish to train them to sell Chevrolets as absolutely the most lavishly appointed automobiles made anywhere in the world. But what we can, and do, train them to believe is that dollar-for-dollar the automobiles and service they sell are one of the *best values* available anywhere in the market.

In a later section, we will zero in on why and how you must focus on value and constantly work to deliver it. Right now, let's consider two of the biggest obstacles you face in delivering value.

Overcoming Two Big Obstacles to Believing in What You Sell

If you are an honest person, you cannot convince a prospect that your product or service has value unless you believe in it yourself. Even if you try, people seem to have an uncanny knack for spotting a phony.

There are two things that most frequently cause salespeople to doubt the value of what they are selling:

First, you cannot believe in what you are selling if you or your company makes false claims for its products, services, or business practices.

Let's face it, the old saying is true: "You can't make a silk purse out of a sow's ear!" No amount of glossing over or looking the other way will convince you that a product has value if you know it will fall apart as soon as it's delivered. Likewise, you cannot believe in your company's services if it consistently fails to deliver what it tells you to promise. If there ever was a time when you could "promise them whatever it takes to close the sale," that time has gone forever.

Your personal reputation with your clients is one of your most valuable assets as a salesperson. You owe it to yourself and your own career to be able to assure your clients of a quality product or service.

Again, being more cautious than Socrates, I don't want to give you a lot of advice. However, I can share how I deal with the problem of value promised but not delivered. First, I don't make claims I know I cannot back up; then I simply refuse to work for anyone who consistently fails to deliver what I'm told to promise clients. I usually confront them with my findings and give them an opportunity to either (1) prove me wrong, (2) correct the abuses, or (3) get themselves another salesperson.

You don't have to work for anybody who knowingly misleads customers. There are far too many honest and upright businesses that are looking for good salespeople for you to squander your reputation on the few who operate unethically.

Second, it is most helpful to realize that all of us perceive values differently.

Let me clarify that statement with an illustration. A young person who is crazy over sports cars loaded with gadgets might find it hard to understand why a conservative older person would be willing to invest good money in a stripped-down sedan, and vice versa. This has strong implications for connecting with your prospect's perceptions of value, as we shall see later.

It's important to see that just because a product or service has little value to you personally doesn't mean it has no value to anyone.

Here's a principle that can help you keep in mind that few things have universal value:

Credibility Principle # 5:
The seller usually determines the cost
of a product or service, but only the
buyer can determine its true value

If you are healthy, you might consider an artificial heart a very poor bargain at $3.98, but if your heart were failing rapidly, you would probably trade everything you had for it. Just because you personally would not pay the asking price for a house is no sign that someone else would not be delighted to get it for that price—even if they knew everything you know about it.

So, if you have difficulty understanding the value of what you are selling, keep in mind that ultimately it is always the buyer who decides how much it is worth to him or her. Remember, "Beauty is in the eye of the beholder."

"If You Ain't Sold, You Can't Sell!"

You can only convince others of the value of what you are selling when *you* are convinced of its value. As salespeople, our task is not to impart value to products that have none, nor even to determine the value of a product to the end user. Our task is to convince our prospects that what we are selling has more value than the money they would pay for it, or anything they could buy with that money.

We can only do that when we are thoroughly convinced of the value of what we are selling. You've got to believe in what you are selling to make your customers believe in what they are buying.

CREDIBILITY FOUNDATION # 4: YOUR PERSONAL INTEGRITY

Early in my selling career, I asked my sales manager about a guy who was selling for us. He told me that he was a drug addict and alcoholic, that bill collectors were always calling the office trying to get money he owed them, that people were always catching him in lies, and that it was usually hard to tell which of the women he ran around with was his current wife. "But I'll tell you one thing," he quickly added, "he's a real closer!" To him, that seemed to make everything else okay. If the guy could close a sale, his personal life was his own business.

The real winners in the selling game—the top 5 percent—know that personal integrity is one of the greatest assets that a salesperson can have. They guard their integrity with a passion.

"Wait a minute!" you might protest. "The way I live my life is my own business!" You're absolutely right! I would not for one minute try to tell you how to live your personal life. In fact, I try to be nonjudgmental in all my dealings. However, my reason for bringing it up is simply this: The way you conduct your business and the way you live your personal life have a direct bearing on your credibility with your customers and prospects. It shows up in many ways:

First, the jump from character (what you are) to reputation (what people think you are) is much smaller than many of us would like to believe. Even people with very low moral principles themselves back away from any salesperson who a colleague tells them is untrustworthy. The issue is not whether it is fair; the issue is that it's a fact of life in selling. Your only defense is absolute integrity.

Second, your character shows up in surprising ways. Shifting or roving eyes, shaky hands, and nervous gestures are like neon signs warning prospects to hold suspect every word you say. Most of us would be surprised how transparent we are to other people.

Third, lying, cheating, and deceiving people are hard to turn on and then turn off—they can easily become habits that shape all our dealings with others. The slightest hint that you can't be trusted can kill more sales than all the efforts you put forth can create.

It Pays Big Dividends to Be Real

Being able to look yourself and others squarely in the eyes, a reputation for being completely trustworthy, and the confidence that comes from never having to fear being found out are worth your own weight in pure gold when it comes to selling. And this leads me to the next big principle for establishing and maintaining your credibility:

> Credibility Principle # 6:
> People pay a lot more attention to what
> you are than to what you say!

The bottom line is that lying, cheating, and loose living can cost you a fortune in customer credibility.

Of course, it's your life, and I can't tell you how to live it. If you can afford it, and are willing to pay the price, you can be as unethical as you choose in all of your dealings. My only reason for bringing it up is that I know what a great asset personal integrity can be to any salesperson who wishes to reach his or her full potential.

TO SUM IT ALL UP...

Credibility—that vital ingredient for successful selling—is never granted; it can only be painstakingly built.

Throughout this whole book, we will be looking at behavior that can help you build trust and confidence in your prospects. This chapter has merely outlined the parameters—the kind of person you are, what you believe, and the way you treat other people.

If you want to see your customer impact soar, test out your own gut feelings about the following:

1. Belief in selling as an honorable profession that is worthy of your best efforts
2. A strong belief in yourself and in your abilities
3. Total confidence in what you are selling and the people you represent
4. Unimpeachable personal integrity

Believe me, if you'll give me a person with all those personal attributes, I can teach that person how to become one of the top salespeople in this country.

ACTION STEPS

Give some thought to how you feel about each of these statements, listing the positives and negatives in each area:

1. I believe that selling is an honorable profession that is worthy of my best efforts.
2. I believe very strongly in myself and in my abilities.
3. I believe very strongly in my company and all its products.
4. Maintaining my personal integrity is one of my highest priorities.

CHAPTER 3

The Greatest Secret
of High Impact Selling

PURPOSE

In this chapter you will discover the greatest secret of high impact selling and how you can use it to

1. Become aware of and sell to your prospect's highest values, allowing them to guide all your selling
2. Uncover your prospect's needs, as he or she perceives them, and use them to profit from selling

"Everyone lives by selling something."
—Robert Louis Stevenson

I. THE MILLION DOLLAR SECRET

We've hinted at it, implied it, and led up to it. Now it's time to share with you the greatest secret of success in selling:

> **The greatest secret in selling:**
> **"Show people what they want most, and**
> **they will move heaven and earth to get it!"**

I wish I could claim credit for that secret because it is so powerful, but it's not original with me. It comes from an anonymous source and was perhaps first revealed in print by Frank Bettger, who learned it from an "old timer" and used its power to make more than a million dollars in selling—in the early years of this century when a million dollars was an enormous amount of money. Let me share with you a story from Mr. Bettger's book, *How I Raised Myself from Failure to Success in Selling*,[1] to show just how powerful the secret is.

As a life insurance salesman, Frank Bettger called on a successful businessman named Scott, and asked him for five minutes of his time, promising to leave after that unless he was asked to stay longer. Mr. Scott agreed but assured him it would be a waste of time for both of them, since he was 63 years old and had long before quit buying insurance. He went on to explain that his children were all grown, his wife was well fixed with paid-up life insurance, his business was well covered, and his estate plan and will were all firmly in place.

Now that would have been enough to send most insurance salespeople packing, but not Frank Bettger. Take a look at what happened next.

"Mr. Scott, a man who has been as successful as you surely must have some interests outside of your family and your business," Mr. Bettger suggested. He had done his homework and knew full well that Mr. Scott was a highly benevolent man who had often given generously to worthwhile causes.

"Perhaps a hospital, religious work, missionary, or charitable work..." he listed a few he knew Mr. Scott had supported. "Did you

---

[1] Frank Bettger, *How I Raised Myself from Failure to Success in Selling* (Englewood Cliffs, N.J.: Prentice-Hall, 1949). Published in paperback by Cornerstone Library, a Simon & Schuster subsidiary of Gulf and Western Corporation, New York, 1979, pp. 33ff.

ever consider that when you die your support will be withdrawn? Wouldn't this loss seriously handicap or even mean the discontinuance of some splendid work?"

At that, the salesman glanced at his watch, noted that his time was up, and thanked his host for his time. Mr. Scott invited him to stay and talk some more. But, again, Frank Bettger was not your typical salesperson. Instead of seizing the opportunity to tell everything he knew about insurance, he started asking questions.

Those questions revealed that the work nearest and dearest to Mr. Scott's heart was the work of three missionary teams in Nicaragua which he supported. He further learned that one of those teams consisted of Mr. Scott's son and daughter-in-law, and that he was planning to visit their work soon.

"Mr. Scott," he finally asked, "when you go down to Nicaragua, wouldn't you be happy to tell your son and his little family that you had just completed arrangements so that, if anything ever happens to you, a check will come to them *every month*, so their work may continue? And wouldn't you like to write a letter to the other two missionaries, giving them the same message?"

There was a long silence; then Mr. Scott thanked Frank Bettger for helping him discover a serious oversight in his planning. No pressure had been applied, and no tricky closes had been used. The old pro had simply shown his prospect what he had wanted most, and the prospect had made a decision to buy. He had not tried to sell insurance; he had shown Mr. Scott that what he really wanted was for the missionary work to continue after he could no longer support it.

After tying down the sale, Frank Bettger walked out of that man's office with a check for $9,000—and that was when $9,000 was a whopping insurance premium. Now that's what I call high impact selling—and it works!

I could introduce you to salespeople who use that secret every day to close sales in almost every business you can name: insurance, automobiles, industrial supplies, real estate, and on and on. What's more, I could introduce you to ten times as many salespeople, in almost any business you can name, who completely ignore that secret and then wonder why they make so few sales.

Let me repeat the secret for you so you'll be sure to remember it:

The Greatest Secret in Selling:
"Show people what they want most, and
they will move heaven and earth to get it!"

I promise you that if you will memorize that simple secret and practice using it on each and every call, it will revolutionize your selling career.

Now let's explore how you can make it work for you.

II. HOW TO CONNECT WITH YOUR PROSPECT'S HIGHEST VALUES

In our last chapter, we discovered that each of us has his or her own value system—we all ascribe certain values to everything that touches our lives.

If you've read my book entitled *High Impact Living*[2] you know that those values are greatly influenced by the subcultures that surround us all our lives, but that each of us has our own unique set of values against which we measure everything.

To connect with your prospect's unique set of values is to establish rapport, to create a climate of trust, and to give your selling proposition a very personal touch. In short, when you discover and identify with your client's own values, it's like saying, "I understand and respect your greatest concerns and interests."

However, to ignore a prospect's value system is to rob yourself of your strongest selling advantage; it's like leaving your most powerful selling tool at home.

The Salesperson's Greatest Folly

Much of sales training has taken the form of inflating salespeople with self-serving slogans and high-sounding selftalk. Not surprisingly, then, connecting with the customer's values is often the last thing on

[2] Bill Brooks, *High Impact Living* (Los Angles: Price/Stern/Sloan, 1987). Copyright 1987 by William T. Brooks.

the mind of the typical salesperson when he or she goes out to sell in the real world.

I once heard about a salesman who went to one of those "enthusiasm rallies" and got so excited about how great he was that he refused to fasten his seatbelt when he boarded the airliner to go home.

"Sir, would you please fasten your seatbelt," the stewardess urged.

"Look at me!" countered the pumped up salesman. "Can't you tell I'm Superman? And Superman don't need no seatbelt!"

"Superman don't need no airplane either, turkey," retorted the stewardess, "so fasten your seatbelt before we throw you off this plane!"

Ridiculous? Of course, it's ridiculous! But it's no more ridiculous than many of the stories I've heard about salespeople who have been brainwashed at sales meetings and then been turned loose on prospects.

"Hi! I'm Mary Smith with XYZ Company. I can see from your left hand that you are a married woman, so let me tell you about a wonderful new perfume that is guaranteed to make your husband sit up and pop both eyes wide open when you walk into the room. May I come in and show you ... !" bubbles the enthusiastic salesperson.

"Good! I hope it will do all you say," says the stunned woman. "My husband just died last night, and I thought you were from the funeral home!"

Trick door openers, canned sales pitches, and speed-talking approaches all thrive on the element of surprise. Unfortunately, it is more often than not the salesperson who gets surprised.

Perhaps that at least partially explains why one-third of all salespeople are looking for different jobs at any given time, and why it is not unusual for sales organizations to have an annual turnover rate of 125 to 175 percent of their sales force.

If sales organizations want to use trick ads to lure unemployed and disillusioned people to "unlimited futures" in selling by intimidation, I guess that is their privilege. What makes me angry about it is that they rob many capable people of their great potential for an honorable selling career. Believe me, if selling has become an unpleasant chore for you because you close so few of the sales you attempt, you may need to look no further than the way you approach prospects.

On the other hand, no matter how successful you have been, you can boost your customer impact and selling power tremendously by using Frank Bettger's secret of showing people what they want most.

How to Make the Values Connection

Before you can show people what they want most, you have to discover what their wants and needs are.

Certainly all people share certain basic needs, interests, and desires. We all want to live, to be loved, to be happy, to have security and adventure. Yet the differences among the ways in which we define those elusive conditions, and our ideas of how to obtain them, are enormous. These different perceptions, and the actions we take to satisfy our desires, are what shape our individual value systems.

How do you connect with a prospect's deepest needs, most compelling interests, and greatest desires? It's a little like staying in good physical condition—relatively simple, but not always easy!

As we shall see in the next section, discovering what people want most involves asking the right questions, listening carefully, and being totally aware of everything that expresses your prospect's values. We'll learn how to master all those skills. However, the important thing now is for you to see how vital they are to your becoming a high impact salesperson and how they can add tremendous power to your persuasion.

III. UTILIZING CUSTOMER NEEDS TO PROFIT FROM VALUE-BASED SELLING

Once you discover what your prospect wants most out of life, you are in an excellent position to utilize value-based selling. It means you can tailor your whole presentation to appeal to that greatest desire—by concerning yourself with what most concerns your prospect. Oddly enough, the reason most people don't custom tailor their presentations is that they say it takes too much time.

First, they feel it takes too much of their own time.

"Man, I don't have time to waste talking to every prospect I see about all those things," a salesperson once said to me. "I have to call on at least 20 people every day to keep my sales up to quota.... You've gotta' get in, tell your story, and get out," she added. "The more people you see, the more money you make ... it's a numbers game. Besides, if people are really interested, they'll buy without all that."

"How many sales a day do you average?" I asked her.

"I always try to make at least two sales a day," she said.

"What if I could show you how to make half as many calls and sell twice as much?... Would you be interested?" I challenged her.

"You bet I would!" she quickly acknowledged.

What she had not yet figured out was that she was closing about 10 percent of the sales she attempted. I shared with her that many of the salespeople I'd trained in value-based selling were closing 40 percent and more of their sales. If she could do that, it meant she could close four sales a day while only calling on ten clients.

I'm not into the numbers game, but those numbers sound pretty good to me!

Second, most salespeople feel their customers don't have time for value-based selling approaches.

"People are busy.... You've got to get right to the point, say what you want to say, and get out," is a fairly typical response to a question I often ask about how much time salespeople spend with their average prospect.

Let me give you a principle of value-based selling:

**Value-Based Selling Principle # 1:
People are always too busy to waste
time doing anything they don't really
want to do!**

We always find time to do what really matters to us. For example, if you're like I am, you can find a thousand ways to avoid spending time in a dentist's chair—unless you happen to have a throbbing toothache. But let one of us get an immobilizing toothache, and we have all the time it takes to go to a dentist.

The nerves you hit through value-based selling may not be as sensitive to your prospects as the ones a dentist hits with pain killer, but the impact can be surprisingly powerful. Whatever time you spend getting in touch with and speaking to your prospect's need will go a long way toward capturing his or her attention and it will pay big dividends for you.

IV. HOW TO CAPTURE YOUR SHARE OF THE MARKET THROUGH VALUE-BASED SELLING

Selling and marketing are not precisely the same thing, although they are very closely related. Selling is actually one of many components that go into making up a company's total marketing system. Yet creative salespeople have discovered they can learn a great deal from at least two types of marketing specialists: marketing research and advertising.

Marketing research concerns itself primarily with finding out what people want, while advertising seeks to interpret how products and services will give people what they want. Both functions are highly sophisticated in today's complex business world, yet the principles behind them are quite simple.

Needs-Satisfaction Selling

Marketing strategists use polls, interviews, and a host of other tools to determine the needs of the people they hope to reach with their products or services. Then the advertising specialists develop ad campaigns to convince potential customers their products or services will meet those needs. It is a highly effective combination.

Yet salespeople have a distinct advantage over marketing specialists: Market research people must rely on generalities, and advertising people must address masses of people with their campaigns— but salespeople can talk in depth with individual prospects. That's one of the biggest reasons salespeople will never be replaced by computers.

What it means is that salespeople can not only explore with people what their needs are, but also determine how each of them perceives those needs. And the perceived need is almost always a more powerful motivation for buying than the actual need is.

Let me illustrate the difference like this. According to management expert Peter Drucker, International Business Machines, Inc., was struggling to survive in the highly competitive office machines market half a century ago. It seemed people had all the business machines they needed and were not interested in buying more from a relatively unknown firm.

The top salespeople in the company took a value-based approach to selling and began to ask their potential customers what they perceived their needs to be. "We need better ways of processing information," came the quick reply.

So the company revamped its whole selling approach. The name of the company was changed to IBM. They called their products "data processing systems and management information systems" instead of office machines, and started providing professional assistance in setting up those systems.

Thus, by addressing their customers' perceived needs, instead of trying only to sell their products, they soon began to dominate the same market they had almost failed at before.

What that means to you as a salesperson is simply this: Once you discover what your prospect perceives his or her most pressing need to be, you can build your whole presentation around that need. It keeps you from wasting precious time on trying to educate customers to needs they may never believe they have, and it puts you in touch with their strongest motivations for buying. It's the difference between trying to create a need and helping the prospect find a much desired solution.

This brings me to a second key principle:

> **Value-Based Selling Principle # 2:**
> **It is always easier to sell to a prospect's**
> **perceived need than to create a need in**
> **the prospect's mind!**

Failure to understand and use that simple principle causes most salespeople to work much harder than necessary, to miss a lot of sales they could close, and to fail when they could succeed at selling.

Value-based salespeople always concern themselves first and foremost with how the prospect perceives his or her needs. Follow along with the text and you will learn how to boost your own persuasive power by needs-satisfaction selling.

Wish-Fulfillment Selling

Some of the most effective value-based selling done in America these days is done by the people who produce commercials for network television. Have you ever noticed that Southern Bell Telephone Company does not ask you to make a long distance call?

Instead, they invite you to "reach out and touch someone." The hamburger chains don't just sell sandwiches; they make appeals such as, "You deserve a break today," and "Have it your way." And the Kodak people don't try to sell you film; they urge you to "Trust your memories to Kodak."

There's a definite reason for using that approach—it works. Some have called it "selling the sizzle instead of the steak," but it involves more than that. It's called "wish-fulfillment selling," and it has some solid psychological reasoning behind it. Studies have shown that if you tell people something they want to believe and you keep repeating it long and often, they will begin to remember it and act upon it.

A major part of the genius behind the private enterprise system is that we have built a vigorous economy by lifting the tastes and quality of life levels of the average citizen. Wish-fulfillment selling has played a major role in that growth and vitality.

Let's face it, in comparison with other cultures, we Americans don't really have that many "needs." Of course, we need food but we don't "need" instant foods in almost every imaginable flavor. What we have done is to sell convenience, simplicity, ease of preparation, reliability, and a host of other intangible values people are willing to pay dearly for. In a nutshell, we've made a fortune by discovering what people want and showing them how to get it through what we are selling. The interesting thing about it all is that typically consumers are not aware that they want all those things, at least until someone shows them that they do.

In fact, most of us would deny that the wish-fulfillment themes used to sell most products have any appeal to us. Yet we continue to buy the products in great quantities. For example, not many of us would go out and buy a "brand X" package of monosodium glutamate, but we will pay extra for the same substance when it's called Accent, because we believe it "wakes up food flavor."

That brings up a very important principle:

> **Value-Based Selling Principle # 3:**
> **All values are equal until someone**
> **points out the difference!**

In value-based selling your task is not merely to show off the features of what you are selling, but to make your prospect believe that what you are selling will fulfill his or her wishes. It takes a lot of creativity, imagination, and an innovative spirit to pull it off; but it is a dynamite sales approach.

How honest is it? It's as honest as you choose to make it. *Integrity selling* demands that you not lead people to expect more than the product can deliver. For example, the most honest thing the cosmetic salesperson who called on a prospect whose husband had just died could do would be to suggest coming back later. There is no perfume or any other substance that could ease the pain of such a loss.

The key to making wish-fulfillment selling work for you is to connect very solidly with the deepest aspirations and hopes of every prospect you call upon, and to know your products and services well enough to see instantly how they can fulfill those desires.

TO SUM IT ALL UP...

In this chapter we have discovered that the greatest secret of high impact selling is:

> "Show people what they want most, and
> they will move heaven and earth to get it!"

We've seen that in order to do that, you have to

1. Connect with and sell to your prospect's highest values
2. Uncover your prospect's needs, as he or she perceives them, and enable your client to meet those needs through what you are selling
3. Connect very solidly with the deepest aspirations and hopes of every prospect you call upon, and know your products and services well enough immediately to identify how they can fulfill those desires

As we have said, this approach is not always easy, but it can help you boost tremendously your customer impact. In our next section, we will present a simple but powerful formula that will enable you to do all these things every time you call upon a prospect.

ACTION STEPS

Set at least three goals for applying what you've read in this chapter to your own selling situation:

_____

_____

_____

Master High Impact Selling Skills

PURPOSE

This section will focus on the science of selling and will provide simple yet powerful strategies to enable you to

1. Develop your own "game plan" of selling
2. Learn an easy-to-remember system which will unlock tremendous selling power for you
3. Apply that selling system to whatever and wherever you are selling

YOU'VE GOTTA' HAVE A PLAN

Motivation without a plan' means only frustration. You set goals for yourself, you push hard to reach them, yet you never seem to get anywhere. You begin to doubt the value of what you are selling, to question your own abilities, and to wonder if you were even cut out to be a salesperson. Sometimes you feel as if you'd rather do anything than approach another prospect.

Or maybe you've been fairly successful, but you've hit a slump; you're on a sales plateau and can't seem to break through to higher selling success.

If you've ever had either of those feelings, I would bet my bottom dollar that you've got one of two problems:

1. You don't have a simple, effective selling system that works well for you, or

2. You are not precisely following that plan.

When I was coaching college football, I discovered that the only way my teams could win consistently was for me to (1) establish a simple, well-conceived "game plan" that took maximum advantage of the unique skills of my players; (2) drill it so firmly into my players' heads that they could follow it without having to think about what they were doing; and (3) insist that it be followed in every detail.

The more I believed in that "game plan," the more my players believed in it, and the more religiously we stuck to it, the more games we would win. It was that simple!

Successful selling is possible by using the exact same formula. If you want to become a consistently high performer in your company or field, you'll find the high impact selling system to be a "game plan" that is both easy to learn and eminently sensible!

Simple to Learn; Easy to Remember

The system contains only six self-evident steps to take you from prospecting to closing the sale, and each step is expressed in a common word or phrase.

- Investigate
- Meet
- Probe
- Apply
- Convince
- Tie it down

Put the first letter of each step together and you get the acronym IMPACT; that's why we call it high impact selling.

High Impact Selling Is Not a Canned Pitch

Canned sales presentations only work with people of below average intelligence. In fact, they are downright insulting to today's educated and alert consumers, many of them professional buyers.

What's more, a stock-in-trade approach completely overlooks the greatest advantage of having a talented salesperson call on prospects—the advantage of one unique human being connecting with another. High impact selling by contrast entails a strategy that can be used by any salesperson to sell anything to any prospect.

"Who needs it?" some will respond. "I just play it by ear." Unfortunately, most of those who say they "play it by ear" actually play it by *mouth* and talk themselves right out of many sales they could close by following a simple, adaptable plan.

A plan has been defined as "a systematic strategy of applied consistency." It's a well-thought-out way of automatically doing the right things, at the right times, and in the right ways.

Once you learn it and practice it a few times, you can do it without having to think about what you are doing. That means you will be free to concentrate on what really matters in closing the sale— the customer.

Adapt; Don't Throw Out the Plan!

Of course every customer is different. The whole first section of this book was designed to show you how important that fact is. So it might sound as if I'm taking the opposite approach by suggesting you follow a system. To help you understand how compatible the two concepts are, let's look again at the football analogy.

Every game our team played was unique. Each opposing team had a different style, the talents of the players varied from team to team, and some of our key players occasionally had "bad days" while others seemed unusually adroit.

The temptation was always there to throw out our basic game plan, either to take advantage of our opponent's weaknesses or to compensate for our own shortcomings. However, we learned the hard way that our surest bet was basically to stick to what we did best and concentrate on doing it even better.

We always prepared for each of our opponents by adapting our plan slightly to compensate for weaknesses and take advantage of our opportunities. For example, if our opponent was weak in passing defense and strong against the run, we might throw a few more passes than usual. Or if our best passing quarterback was injured, we would run a little more often. However, our basic game plan covered every aspect of the game, and it always stayed the same.

That's exactly what I'm suggesting that you do in selling. Adopt the high impact selling system as your basic game plan, then adapt it to take advantage of opportunities and compensate for problems.

Let me illustrate it with an example. Suppose you know a prospect very well, and consider him or her a personal friend. Obviously, you won't have to spend as much time in the Meeting step, which includes establishing rapport with the prospect. Instead you will be able to move quickly into the Interview step.

A word of caution, however: since the selling situation is quite different from a social call, it is generally not too helpful to behave in too casual a manner with persons you already know. So you will want to adapt your meeting strategies to enable you to set up the ideal selling situation. You don't throw out the step; you just adapt it to fit the situation in which you are selling.

The High Impact Selling System:
A Brief Overview

A system only makes sense when you can see the whole plan and understand how each part fits into the broader picture. Before we move on to give you a clear picture of how to do each step, let's look over the whole system and see how it fits together.

Remember, the system contains six steps: Investigate, Meet, Probe, Apply, Convince, and Tie it up. To boost your IMPACT with your prospects and clients, use the following outline as a guide in studying the remainder of the text.

- INVESTIGATE:

Functions:
1. To give you a large range of qualified prospects for what you are selling
2. To give you all the information you need about those prospects to be most convincing
3. To enable you to prepare your strongest and most persuasive presentation

- MEET:

Functions:
1. To set up the best selling situation
2. To make your prospects feel important and relaxed
3. To start them talking about themselves
4. To gain rapport

- PROBE:

Functions:
1. To discover what your potential clients want most
2. To uncover real and perceived needs
3. To get them involved in the selling process
4. To assess their buying styles

- APPLY:

Functions:
1. To show prospective buyers that you understand their needs and desires
2. To present the product or service that will fulfill those needs and desires
3. To let them experience how the product or service will meet theirneeds%desires
4. To make sure they understand what benefits they will receive from ownership

- CONVINCE:

Functions:
1. To validate and prove every claim you have made
2. To answer any questions prospective buyers may have
3. To justify the price by emphasizing value

4. To reemphasize the importance of customers' desires and relieve any fears of buying

● TIE IT UP:

Functions:
1. To negotiate a win–win agreement
2. To welcome, identify, and answer all objections
3. To reinforce customers' positive feelings about buying
4. To close the sale
5. To get referrals and introductions

You probably are already implementing many of these individual steps, but the high impact selling system provides a convenient plan for doing them in the most powerful way. Each step sets up the next one and steadily moves the prospect to a buying decision without making him or her feel pressured in any way.

Take It One Step at a Time

You don't have to learn all these selling behaviors in one sitting or start doing them all at once. This method has worked for thousands of salespeople to double, or even triple, their sales—one step at a time.

The best way to learn this comprehensive new system is to break it down into bite-sized chunks and digest it through repeated reading and practice. As you carefully digest one step, you can move on to the next one.

You will begin almost immediately to notice a sharp rise in your closing average. Within a few weeks, you will have learned the system so well you can do each of the steps without having to think about it. When that happens, you will see your customer impact and sales soar.

And so, let's begin. . . . We'll start with Step 1—Investigate.

CHAPTER 4

Step One: Investigate

How to Find and Prepare for Plenty of Prospects

PURPOSE

In Step One, we'll learn how to set up successful sales by:

1. Power-packed prospecting
2. Gathering information that can help you close sales

> *"A wise man will make*
> *more opportunities*
> *than he finds."*
>   *—Francis Bacon*

I. PROSPECTING: WHERE THE ACTION BEGINS

"Bill, I want you to come in here and teach these knuckleheads how to close a sale!" a frustrated sales manager once told me.

"Are you sure closing is the problem?" I asked.

"I know my salespeople are not lazy," he explained. "They talk to a lot of people every day, they make a lot of pitches, and I see to it they know their products. . . . They just don't get people to sign on the dotted line!"

"But do they see the right people, and are they really ready when they go on a sales call?" I asked.

"What do you mean?" he retorted.

That's when I explained to him that the most vital part of a sale is seldom the close but *what takes place before the interview begins.*

After I'd done a careful study of his situation and talked with several of his salespeople, I concluded that their problem was not that they didn't know how to close sales—most of the sales interviews they were conducting were not potential sales to start with. Their problem was they didn't know how to *open* sales.

Sure, they would "go out and find the people," and certainly they would "lay a mean sales pitch on anybody who would listen to them long enough." They were extremely busy all the time, and they were remarkably effective at getting in to see people. What's more, they knew how to use every closing technique in the book.

Most of them had been trained under the old school that said, "If you tell your story to enough people, some of them will buy." Unfortunately, there just weren't enough hours in the day for them to succeed.

You should have seen that sales manager's eyes pop out when I suggested we do a seminar on prospecting for all his salespeople. But you should have seen the smile on his face six months after the seminar when he told me how sales had risen sharply right after that—and had been climbing steadily ever since.

II. POWER-PACKED PROSPECTING

The real issue is not how often you tell your story, but to whom and how you tell your story. It's the difference between looking everywhere for opportunities and creating your own opportunities.

Now I'm not suggesting for one minute that you can be successful at selling by sitting on your duff all day. Good prospecting is hard work. In fact, most salespeople find it easier to run around and shoot off their mouths than they do to approach pre-sale investigating as a science and work at it consistently. But the better job of prospecting and preparing you do, the better your chances of closing more sales.

Prospecting as Investigation

"But investigation sounds like work for a detective!" you may protest. That's not a bad comparison—not bad at all. A good detective always follows several guidelines that are equally applicable to prospecting by salespeople:

1. A good detective always looks beyond the obvious, but never overlooks the obvious.
2. A good detective always asks a lot of questions.
3. A good detective follows a set plan.
4. A good detective makes detailed notes and keeps accurate, up-to-date records.
5. A good detective uses every means available to check out every possibility.
6. A good detective manages time carefully so he or she is always at the right place, doing the right thing, at the right time.
7. A good detective follows up every lead.

As you can see, a wise salesperson does everything a good detective does, and even more.

In Search of Qualified Prospects

However, there is a significant difference in the goals salespersons versus detectives are aiming at. A detective is looking for one guilty *suspect*, but the salesperson is looking for as many qualified *prospects* as possible.

In selling, a suspect is a person:

1. You've opened limited communications with
2. Who may have a need you can satisfy, although he or she may not yet know it
3. Who may or may not have the resources to buy
4. Who may or may not listen to you

But a qualified prospect is a person:

1. You've established some rapport with
2. Who has a need you can satisfy, and knows it
3. Has the resources to satisfy that need
4. Has agreed to listen to you

Many salespeople spend their most productive selling time—their prime time—trying to sell suspects, instead of making presentations to qualified prospects. Unfortunately, your closing average with suspects will always be much lower than it would be for the same amount of time invested with qualified prospects.

This suggests a very important principle:

> Prospecting Principle # 1:
> The better job of finding qualified
> prospects you do, the higher your
> closing average will be!

You can significantly boost your selling impact simply by making it a habit to spend all your prime selling time with the most qualified prospects you can find. To do that, you will need to readjust your schedule by using "peripheral time" to search for suspects and to try to move them to the category of qualified prospects.

For example, if your prime selling time is from 9:00 AM until 4:00 PM, you could spend two hours before and two hours after that period each day trying to make prospects out of suspects. If the lunch period is not a good selling time for your clientele, why not invest that 60 to 90 minutes in taking suspects to lunch or doing other follow-up work?

III. SIX TOOLS TO HELP YOU FIND PLENTY OF QUALIFIED PROSPECTS

During hundreds of training sessions and consultations with scores of business leaders, I have found unanimous agreement on one basic point: Lack of qualified prospects is the greatest single cause of failure among salespeople.

Prospecting is the toughest part of selling. It means more than merely finding warm bodies you might corral into listening to your pitch. It includes finding a sizable number of qualified prospects, establishing enough rapport with them to gain a good hearing, and setting the stage (time and place) for you to make your best presentations.

We've seen how prospecting is similar to detective work, but there is another profession even more closely analogous to prospecting: investigative reporting.

A sharp investigative reporter always uses six tools to track down a story—Who? Where? What? Why? When? and How?—tools just as useful to the alert salesperson who is committed to the job of prospecting.

That brings up the second principle of prospecting:

> **Prospecting Principle # 2:**
> **The salesperson who asks enough of the right questions, of the right persons, in the right places, will always have plenty of qualified prospects.**

Let's explore how these six tools of prospecting can work for you. I can only give you general ideas that will work in many fields of selling. Your task is to apply them to your own selling situation.

Prospecting Tool # 1: Who?

An investigative reporter in a city of a million people will get nowhere if he or she assumes that every resident in the city is a likely candidate for a story. Rather the reporter has to start narrowing down the field to those whose stories are truly newsworthy and then choose a few to focus on in depth.

In prospecting, some very good *who* questions to keep asking are:

1. Who has the most obvious need or desire for what I'm selling? For whom is that need or desire most compelling?
2. Who are my ideal prospects? (Describe them in detail.)
3. Who do I know that might fit that description?
4. Who do I know that might lead me to people who fit that description?
5. Who has the money to buy what I'm selling?
6. Who has bought similar products or services before?
7. Who has bought from me or my company, but might be ready to buy again?

If you approach this task creatively, you can develop a huge suspect list from those questions alone, but the key is to keep asking them over and over again, and to constantly look for names you might have missed.

Prospecting Tool # 2: Where?

By asking enough *where* questions, you can turn up prospects beyond your family, friends, and business associates. You'll be amazed at how many lists of people you can find, many of whom will be logical prospects.

Here are some sample *where* questions that produce great results:

1. Where do my ideal prospects live? Work? Play? Worship? Socialize? Relax?
2. Where can I find useful mailing lists of people who fit my ideal prospect description? (If you scout around a little, you can find lists of people by professions, neighborhoods, types and frequency of purchases, credit ratings, automobile registrations, property deeds, and so on.)
3. Where can I find directories from which I can assemble my own lists? (Places to look would include the business section of your public library, clubs, social groups, officers and directors of service organizations, for example.)

4. Where might I go to make contact with prospects? (Consider places like country clubs, health and recreation centers, exhibits and shows.)

Our society has gone bonkers over lists of people, and computers have made it possible for those lists to be arranged by very convenient categories. The more careful you are in selecting your lists, the more productive they will be for you.

Prospecting Tool # 3: Why?

Why questions can help you prioritize your time as you seek to transform suspects into prospects. They can also help you determine which approach is best to reach a particular person or group of people.

The following *why* questions are helpful:

1. Why would this person be most likely to buy from me?
2. Why would this person resist buying?
3. Why might this time be especially good (or poor) to approach this person?
4. Why would this person be most likely to give me a hearing? (If your answer to this one is that they would respond to a referral, can you get a referral?)

You have to watch your attitude when you are doing this kind of questioning. If you approach the *why* questions negatively, they can talk you out of calling on anybody, but if you approach them positively, they will help you determine who should get top priority and what approach to use.

Prospecting Tool # 4: What?

The family of *what* questions can enable you to boost your prospecting impact by helping you focus on your most powerful content for prospecting.

Here are a few you might find helpful:

1. What will this prospect find most attractive about my product or service?

2. What will he or she find least attractive?

3. What questions or statements are most likely to get prospects' attention?

4. What more do I need to know about the person to assure success in setting up an appointment?

5. What information should I try to gain from my initial contact with the prospect?

Obviously you will only want to invest time asking the *what* questions to people you consider likely prospects, but the higher the quality of your answers to those questions, the greater your batting average will be in getting appointments.

Prospecting Tool # 5: When?

Timing has a great influence on how successful you will be at prospecting. Too often, salespeople try to set up appointments for their own convenience rather than at an optimum time for the prospect. Others have so few prospects that they jump at an appointment any time they can get one.

A more positive and productive approach is to blend your interests with those of the prospect and always shoot for the best time schedule for both of you.

Questions like these can help you do just that:

1. When is the optimum time for me to do my prospecting and not cut into my prime time?

2. When is it most productive (from the customer's viewpoint) for me to try to contact suspects? When is it least productive?

3. When is this prospect most likely to give me a good, solid hearing? When is the best time for me? When is a good alternate time for both of us?

4. When should I contact this prospect again if my first efforts are not successful?

Salespeople who are most successful try both to practice good time management habits and also to work toward getting quality appointments. For example, they know it is seldom productive to see a busy executive first thing on Monday morning, so they try to schedule other types of clients for that time.

Prospecting Tool # 6: How?

How questions are perhaps the most crucial of all the tools for prospecting. Many of their answers will evolve from answers to the five other types of questions, but there are some *how* questions you'll find very helpful:

1. How can I make more time for prospecting without cutting into my prime selling time?
2. How can I utilize my prospecting time more productively, including the few moments available to me right now?
3. How can I sharpen my prospecting skills?
4. How can I best approach suspects and prospects—especially this one?
5. How can I be sure I'm doing a good enough job of follow-up in prospecting?

Again, the key to making the *how* questions work for you is to keep asking them and revising your answers.

A Backward Glance

"He that questioneth much shall learn much," said Francis Bacon. Nowhere is that statement more true than in prospecting. I've shared with you some of the kinds of questions I constantly ask myself—questions that have helped me to eliminate completely the problem of not having a qualified prospect to call on at any given moment.

Let me sum up what we have learned about the task of prospecting so far:

Prospecting Principle # 3:
The most productive sentence in the
salesperson's vocabulary always ends
with a question mark!

Good prospecting is a matter of developing a solid game plan that works well for you and following that game plan to the letter. Let me give you some pointers to help you formulate your own game plan.

IV. PROSPECTING POINTERS

The following ideas for productive prospecting have been tested and proven effective by leading salespeople in all fields. Look them over and see how you can apply them to your own selling situation:

1. Treat prospecting as the lifeblood of your sales career:
   a. Focus on quantity. Your success depends on having enough solid sales leads.
   b. Focus on quality. It's the only way you can spend most of your prime time with qualified prospects.
   c. Focus on consistency. A steady supply of qualified prospects can enable you to avoid slumps and plateaus, call reluctance, and putting undue pressure on clients.
   d. Do it now. Increasing your prospecting effectiveness is the fastest single way to boost your sales and income.
2. Treat prospecting as your most valuable time management tool:
   a. Use it to avoid wasting prime time on people who are not qualified to say "yes."
   b. Use it to ensure that you will always have enough qualified prospects to keep you productively busy.
   c. Avoid time wasting through sloppy or haphazard prospecting.
3. Take an organized approach. Avoid keeping leads on scraps of paper stuck everywhere. You can buy a computerized system or create one of your own, but make sure it enables you to avoid

    a. Losing or forgetting about valuable leads

    b. Being late on promised follow-ups

    c. Wasting time looking for lost information

    d. Not properly valuing your prospect inventory

    e. Failing to do mailings and other footwork because of the disorder of your prospect list

    f. Becoming a compulsive procrastinator when it comes to working with your prospect inventory

4. Always keep on the alert for prospects:

    a. Develop a prospecting mind set that automatically asks, "Is this person a prospect?"

    b. Assume all suspects are prospects until proven otherwise.

    c. Keep looking for new places to look for prospects.

    d. Cultivate mutually beneficial relationships with all people who can give you leads or open doors for you.

    e. Take full advantage of every effort by your company to generate leads.

    f. Work as much as you can on referrals from satisfied customers.

5. Stay in constant touch with active prospects through phone calls, periodic mailings, and personal contacts. Keep in mind the "Top of the Consciousness Principle" which states that:

    a. Others are always competing for your prospect's attention and dollars.

    b. You never know when your prospect's motivation to buy will suddenly, dramatically increase.

    c. You need to be sure that he or she thinks of your product first, if and when he or she decides to buy.

    d. The only certain way to ensure you are thought of first is through frequent, repetitious contact.

6. Rework your suspect inventory regularly to try to upgrade suspects to the status of qualified prospects:

    a. Learn to use the telephone in a professional, pleasant, and business-like manner and use it regularly.

    b. Constantly search for a person who can give you a referral for each suspect or—better yet—make contact for you.

     c. Look everywhere for the slightest clue that the person's buying status might be changing.

7. Keep upgrading your prospecting system and techniques:
   a. Read, listen to cassettes, attend seminars, and talk to other successful salespeople to get ideas you can use.
   b. If you are not now using a personal computer, consider buying one. It can be an incredible aid in prospecting and managing prospect information files. Make sure you get a system that will work easily and well for you and will grow with your needs.
   c. Above all, keep a positive attitude about prospecting. Make a game out of it. Remember, it is the lifeblood of your selling career.

TO SUM IT ALL UP...

In the first section of the book, we discovered that the greatest secret of high impact selling is:

> "Show people what they want most, and they will move heaven and earth to get it!"

But before you can show people what they want, you have to find people who can get in touch with their needs/desires and fulfill them through what you are selling. That's what prospecting is all about. It's what makes prospecting the most vital step in the selling process.

Prospecting is not simply finding "suckers" you might rope into listening to you spout off the virtues of what you are selling. It is finding a sufficient quantity of qualified prospects who have a need and desire for what you are selling and who have the authority and financial resources to satisfy that desire.

The high impact selling system calls it Investigating, because it not only involves finding qualified prospects but includes finding out everything you can to help you close the sale—before you move to the second step.

Once you have made a thorough investigation to obtain all the information you can about a qualified prospect, you are ready for that all-important second step: You are ready to Meet your prospect.

ACTION STEPS

List at least three ways you can apply the "investigative" techniques outlined in this chapter to your own prospecting:

_____

_____

_____

CHAPTER 5

Step Two: Meet

How to Turn Sales Resisters into Active Listeners

PURPOSE

The purpose of this chapter is to show you how to break down mental barriers and get your prospects involved as active participants in what you want to happen. You'll discover how to:

1. Get people to lower their mental/emotional defenses and let you in
2. Eliminate tension and establish trust
3. Build rapport
4. Start successful sales talk

> *All effective sales talk is dialog!*

HOW TO GET PEOPLE INVOLVED IN WHAT YOU WANT TO HAPPEN

When you meet someone, you "make personal contact with," you "enter into personal dealings with" them, or you "come together from different directions."

That's precisely what must happen before selling can begin. It means more than the casual introduction and handshaking we normally associate with "meeting" people. Its backbone is a specific approach, but it also involves fleshing that out.

In the Meeting step of high impact selling, your goals are to:

1. Become personally acquainted with your prospect
2. Establish a strong trust bond between you and your prospect
3. Build a warm and cordial rapport with each other
4. Set the selling process in motion

The old school of sales training spoke of this as "the warmup," and thought of it as "setting them up for the kill." The idea was that you would tell a few jokes; then, while they were in a good mood, you'd move in for the close, get your money, and split. Any salesperson who tries that approach with today's sophisticated consumer or professional buyer is in for a rude awakening.

My father-in-law is a beef farmer in Virginia, and I've learned a great deal about selling from watching the way he responds to the many salespeople who drop by from time to time while I'm visiting with him on the farm.

A true "Southern gentleman," he will go out of his way to be hospitable and will even chuckle at their jokes. But the moment they make their first sales overture, he gets that glassy-eyed look on his face and withdraws into his own little world. Almost always, the salespeople who try the old "warmup" routine on him fail to get to first base.

I've also noticed, however, that salespeople who show a genuine interest in getting acquainted with him, and who meet him in his world of farming, find him willing to listen to almost anything they have to say.

I. HOW TO GET PEOPLE TO DROP EVERYTHING AND LISTEN TO YOU

Sometimes selling feels almost combative. All too often it degenerates into a "we/they" situation, a war of the wills in which everybody loses.

But it doesn't have to be that way. Markita Andrews set a world record in selling at the ripe old age of 12. In one three-week period, she contacted more than 1,500 prospects and sold 3,516 boxes of Girl Scout cookies—more than anyone has ever sold. That phenomenal achievement gained for her:

- A starring role in a sales training film
- A number of TV appearances
- A place in the *Guiness Book of World Records*
- A visit to the White House
- A great deal of personal satisfaction

Certainly, Markita represented a solid and popular organization and had a good product that was both in strong demand and had a powerful emotional appeal. But so did all the thousands of other girls who were selling Girl Scout cookies, yet none of them even came close to her record.

She attributes her success to three things:

1. A clear-cut personal goal
2. Making a lot of contacts
3. A simple, honest sales approach

"But I'm not a cute little girl selling goodies to a sympathetic market!" one industrial salesman protested. "I'm in a dog-eat-dog market, where they chew up salespeople and spit them out for recreation!"

Granted, it is not always easy to break through the sales resistance, competitive demands, and frantic pace of life to get people to listen to you. But the fact that thousands of successful salespeople all over America do it every day is proof enough that it's possible. What's more, their success proves that those sales winners do more than just get a foot into the door—they get people involved in what they want to happen.

That's the whole purpose of the Meeting phase of the high impact selling system—to change prospects from defenders against your selling efforts into active participants in the selling process.

II. HOW TO ELIMINATE TENSION AND ESTABLISH TRUST

Let's face it, most people see a sales call as an interruption from the important things they want to (or feel they ought to) be doing. A salesperson is often viewed as an intruder, a money-grabber, and sometimes even a beggar. At best, many polite prospects tend to see themselves as being nice to a fellow human, or actually doing you a favor. Unless you can change that basic attitude and atmosphere, you're a dead duck before you get started.

What that means to you is that, before selling can begin, tension must be greatly reduced or eliminated. Prospects must come to feel that you are a trustworthy person, that you have something important to say to them, and that they might benefit enough to justify the time they invest in listening to you.

That's a big order, isn't it? But let's add one more dimension to make it even bigger. You have to accomplish all that in a matter of minutes—sometimes even in seconds.

Let's take a look at two very effective strategies used regularly by the real pros in this business.

1. First, You Have to Win the Inner Game

Prospects can read you like a book. They can instantly sense your confidence level, your attitude about selling and what you are selling, your feelings toward them, and your personal comfort level at being with them. It shows in your eyes, your gestures and movements, and even in your tone of voice.

You simply can't consistently fake your way through the inner game of selling and be a winner in the outer game. We devoted all of Chapter 2 to this crucial issue of winning the inner game of selling, but it is so vital to your success I feel compelled to reemphasize it here.

"But I can't change the way I think and feel!" you protest. I've got good news for you! You can change even your most basic attitudes and thoughts. It starts when you begin replacing your negative, self-limiting thoughts with positive thoughts and insights.

If you want to experience a real change in the ways prospects see you, start feeding positive thoughts into your mind—thoughts like these:

- Selling is an honorable profession that is worthy of my best efforts.
- My purpose for being here is to enable this person to discover what he or she wants most, and how to get it.
- I am a value generator for this person and all my clients. I concentrate on value and seek to deliver it.
- The company I represent is a solid firm that seeks to deliver greater value than it receives in payment for its products and services.
- What I'm selling has a greater value to people than the money they will pay for it. I will see to it that they get what they pay for, and more.
- I am a capable and confident salesperson.
- I will not rely upon high pressure to make this sale, but will concentrate on making a high impact upon this customer.
- When I finish this interview, I will leave behind a happy customer who will feel good about me and my company.

Not one of those is an artificial claim that you cannot back up with facts. If you have a problem believing any of them, let me urge you to work through them until you can honestly say them to yourself.

When you start seeing yourself in that light, you'll be happily surprised at how much more warmly your prospects will receive you.

2. Creating Trust

The natural condition that exists at the beginning of any selling situation is tension, even when your prospects are close friends or relatives. We could talk for days about all the factors that cause such tension, but you've probably experienced enough of it to know how real it is.

The fact is that tension will exist until you take action to reduce or eliminate it. So let's focus on what you can do about it. Here are three techniques I've found to be very helpful:

First, eliminate any unnecessary tension inducers before you make the sales call. That includes things like being neat in appearance and dressed in a manner that will make your prospects feel you are one of them.

"This is a free country," a novice salesperson once told an old pro. "I can dress as I please, wear my hair as I please, and drive any kind of car I choose; and no one can stop me!"

"You're right!" responded the seasoned veteran, "And that prospect can exercise his freedom to say 'no'; and nobody can stop him!"

All you need do is notice how you react to the way strangers look and you will agree how important it is to make a good first impression.

Second, look for tangible ways to help your clients relax. A quiet manner, a mild sense of humor, and a warm smile can go a long way toward breaking down barriers between you and your prospects.

A short, humorous personal story that identifies you as "ordinary folks" can often do wonders to help people relax, especially if you listen while they tell you a story of their own in return.

However, be extremely careful about telling jokes. Most people don't tell a lot of jokes, and they feel uncomfortable around salespeople who do. Besides, it takes special skill to tell jokes that really go over big with everyone.

For the same reasons, I would suggest you also use one-liners very cautiously. If you start out by telling a big joke or set up a series of one-liners and nobody laughs, where do you go from there? Unless you have a ready sense of humor that most people can easily identify with, concentrate on selling and leave the joking to comedians.

Third, be a good guest. When you are in someone's home or workplace you're on their turf, and you are bound by etiquette and common courtesy to observe the "house rules."

For example, you might feel quite comfortable putting your feet on a coffee table, but if you do that with some prospects, they will immediately identify you as insensitive and start looking for ways to get rid of you.

Smoking cigarettes is a real turn-off with many people these days, and a cigar is almost never acceptable. If you smoke, I would strongly suggest you not light up unless your host does—and then only after asking permission.

On the more positive side, one of the best ways to gain trust is to graciously receive any hospitality your hosts offer. To many people, offering a drink or snack is a way of saying, "Let's be friends." To turn it down is like saying, "No! I'd rather be a stranger."

Remember, tension is the natural state that exists in the selling situation. It won't just go away on its own. You have to take positive steps to create the kind of trust which eliminates or reduces the tension before you can begin selling.

III. BUILD RAPPORT BY GETTING PEOPLE ACTIVELY INVOLVED

Have you ever tried to talk your way out of a traffic ticket while the officer just kept on writing? He may half listen and occasionally nod his head, but he just keeps on inexorably writing that ticket. Of course, you may not be able to talk him out of the fine anyway, but you certainly won't make any progress until you can get him to stop what he's doing and pay attention to what you are trying to tell him.

It's the same way with selling. You can't begin selling until people start listening to you, and they won't listen to you until they really want to hear what you have to say. In short, you have to get their attention and pique their interest.

The best way to gain clients' attention is to get them actively involved in what you want to happen. Here are some tested and proven techniques for doing just that:

First, the quickest way to get people involved with you is to get involved with them.

Early in my direct selling experience, I saw an old pro do this. He was making a presentation to a family with a three-year-old boy who was a terror. The father was about half listening and half watching TV, the little boy was dismantling the salesman's brief case, and the mother was busy trying to keep the child under control. I expected the old salesman to give up at any moment and beat a hasty retreat.

But, was I in for a surprise! Almost before I knew what was happening, the guy was sitting on the floor, asking the little fellow to help him find a book in the sales kit. Soon he was reading a story from the book, and the little boy was sitting in rapt attention and sheer delight.

The father seemed amazed that his little terror would sit still to hear a story and was soon deeply involved in what was going on. The mother relaxed and started asking questions. Within a matter of minutes, we left that house with a check and a signed order.

That salesman knew the most important thing in that couple's life was the little guy, so he found a way to get the whole family involved—and he did it by getting involved with the object of their affection.

It takes a great deal of creativity, but you can always turn a distraction into a common meeting ground. If something is important enough to your prospects to distract them, it also has the potential for getting them involved with you.

Second, gain eye contact and plug into the emotions of your prospect.

This is a powerful lesson that I learned from my close associate, Ron Willingham, author of *Best Seller* (Prentice-Hall).

Try to connect with what the person is feeling: about your being there, about other things going on in his or her life at the moment, and about life in general.

Put yourself in that person's shoes and try to pick up on what he or she is experiencing at the moment. For example, if the person has a headache, imagine what it would be like to listen to a salesperson talk while your head was throbbing.

When you do that, two amazing things happen. You begin to actually feel a genuine empathy with what the person is feeling, and the empathy you feel is somehow transmitted through the eye contact to the other person.

One of the best ways to get people involved with what you want to happen is to feel and show a real understanding of what they are feeling.

Third, ask your clients questions to get them involved in talking about themselves.

Nothing gets a prospect involved in the selling process more quickly or effectively than inviting them to talk about themselves. Most people will talk with you about themselves even if they won't talk with you about anything else.

There are three keys to making it work:

1. Ask questions that draw them out. "That's a beautiful plant. Have you been raising houseplants long?"

2. Really listen to what they say. Looking a person straight in one eye and paying attention to everything they say is one of the most effective ways to show you are interested in them as human beings. Besides, it provides a great opportunity for you to pick up insights that will help you sell.

3. Show a genuine interest in what they tell you by feeding it back to them. "I'm sure you're very concerned that your neighborhood is changing so dramatically."

I've given you only three techniques for getting people involved in what you want to happen. I'm sure, with a little imagination, you can come up with many other ways that apply directly to your own situation.

What's really important is that you do whatever it takes to build rapport—to get them actively involved in the selling process. No real selling can take place until that happens.

IV. HOW TO START SUCCESSFUL SALES TALK

The final stage of the Meeting step of high impact selling is to introduce the subject you want to occupy center stage of the session with your prospect, namely, selling your product.

Shifting gears to sales talk can be very awkward, both for you and your prospect. In fact, many of the salespeople who've attended my seminars have confessed that this is the most uncomfortable part of the whole interview for them.

Setting the Stage for Action, not for Reaction

The shift from friendly conversation to active sales talk is one you simply must make, but when you make it, you want response— not reaction.

Perhaps the most helpful image that comes to mind is building a bridge across a chasm. The best way to move prospects from friendly chitchat to businesslike sales talk is to give them a firm foundation to walk across.

Obviously, the most crucial factor in building a bridge is knowing where you're going from and what your destination is. One reason so many salespeople fail at building that bridge is that they start from the wrong place and/or try to get to the wrong place. They may start from a tricky foot-in-door tactic and try to set the prospect for the kill. It just doesn't work. A better approach is to start from a position of strong trust and good rapport, then build the bridge to conveying value. I won't say much about either of those positions, for two reasons:

First, we've spent most of your time and my space so far talking about how important it is to create a strong trust bond.

Second, if you don't see yourself as conveying value to your prospects by selling whatever it is you sell, you need to go back and spend some time practicing the inner game of selling. Nothing I can tell you about building bridges will help until you resolve that issue within yourself.

Instead, I want to give you some pointers on how the real winners in the sales game build that bridge from trust and rapport to conveying value.

1. *Get to the point of your visit quickly.*

Four things are uppermost in the prospect's mind from the moment you knock at the door: (1) Who are you? (2) Whom do you represent? (3) What do you want? (4) What's in it for me?

The quicker you can answer those questions, the sooner they can relax and get on with sales talk.

2. *Avoid being abrupt.*

Amateurs often say things like: "Well, I know you folks don't have all day to talk and neither do I, so let's get down to business." Or they may ask a startling question that is totally out of touch with everything that's been said up to that point.

But the real pros take a more gentle approach. They ask non-threatening questions or make statements that gently open the door.

3. *Make it natural.*

Let it flow naturally from the rapport you've set in motion. Look for a tangible way to identify with the prospect and start from there. Search for a common interest, a point of personal pride or delight for the prospect, or a way to express concern over a problem he or she might be experiencing, and use that as a launching pad for your shift into sales talk.

Things have a way of becoming intensely interesting to us when they become personal. Likewise, salespeople become very interesting to prospects when they become personal in a nonthreatening way. But by all means don't be artificial with it. False flattery, inane chatter, and insincere comments create tension rather than reduce it.

Nor am I suggesting you fake an interest you don't have. If you are not genuinely interested in people, you'll have a tough time making a living in sales. But if you are really interested, all you need do is use a little creativity to find a way to express it.

By identifying with your prospects, you enable them to identify with you. You help to establish the feeling that you see life pretty much as they do, and that you mean them no harm.

4. *Test your bridge before you invite the client to walk across.*

Many jolly and talkative prospects suddenly lapse into morbid seriousness or a deathly silence at the first effort to move toward sales talk. Then, too, a congenial prospect can suddenly turn into an aggressive attacker. When one of those two things happens, you know instantly you haven't built a strong enough trust bond.

Prospects often resist sales talk because they have been subjected to so much high pressure from manipulative salespeople that they are afraid to ask a question, volunteer any information, or show any sign of interest.

For those reasons, it is important constantly to test the trust you have established. One of the most effective ways to do this is to introduce sales talk in stages and watch closely for reactions.

You might ask for a simple piece of information, then monitor carefully how freely the information is given. If you get a warm and immediate response, you know it is safe to proceed. But if you sense reluctance, it's better to back up and build more trust rather than add to the growing tension.

TO SUM IT ALL UP...

All effective sales talk is dialog. To dialog with people is to "get in touch" with them in a meaningful way—to set in motion a two-sided conversation which demonstrates that you value them, their feelings, and their needs.

Unless you (1) get people to lower their mental/emotional defenses and let you in, (2) eliminate tension and establish trust, (3) build rapport, and (4) start successful sales dialog, you cannot move forward to make the sale. All these actions are part of the crucial Meeting step of the high impact selling system.

Next we'll explore how to (1) tune in to your prospects' perceptions of their needs, (2) make them aware of some unrecognized needs, and (3) let your questions do the selling for you.

ACTION STEPS

Set goals for boosting your effectiveness in the Meeting step by taking action in each of the following areas:

1. Get people to lower their mental/emotional defenses and let you in.
   GOAL: _____

2. Eliminate tension and establish trust.
   GOAL: _____

3. Build rapport.
   GOAL: _____

4. Start successful sales dialog.
   GOAL: _____

CHAPTER 6

Step Three: Probe

How to Help
People Discover
What They Want Most

PURPOSE

The Probe step is the core of the high impact selling system. You'll discover in this chapter how to show people what they want most by:

1. "Listening" people into buying instead of talking your way out of the sale
2. Discovering what they will buy, why they will buy it, and under what conditions they will buy it
3. Enabling them to focus their needs and wants in their own minds

> *"Buy my English posies*
> *And I'll sell your heart's desire!"*
> *—from "The Flowers"*
> *by Rudyard Kipling*

MEASURE YOUR PROSPECTS—DON'T JUST SIZE THEM UP

Imagine what it would be like if doctors acted like many salespeople. You might walk into a doctor's office one day and be greeted with a scenario like this.

"Boy, are you in luck today!" he'd greet you.

"I don't feel so lucky . . . my head hurts like crazy!" you respond.

"Know why you're lucky?" he asks, ignoring your comment. "We're running a block-busting close-out sale on artificial hearts . . . getting ready for the new models!"

"But, Doc," you protest, "it's my head that hurts, not my heart."

"Yessir! I can fix you up with this 'Super Pumper' model, which is loaded with options, for the unbelievably low price of $40,000 . . . . That's a 40 percent savings . . . . Besides, it's all covered by your insurance. Could I schedule you for installation Tuesday, or would Thursday be more convenient for you?"

If you are like most of us you would run—not walk—to the nearest exit.

I don't want to belabor the point by stretching the scenario further, and I don't want to leave the impression I think all salespeople are that insensitive. But sometimes it helps to look at a ridiculous example in order to detect a fatal flaw in our own selling patterns.

The Fatal Flaw in Selling

As one who trains hundreds of salespeople every year, I have observed that most salespeople talk their way out of more sales than they listen their way into. People who subscribe to the "jawbone theory" of selling lose many sales they could make because they focus more on what *they* want to happen than on what *their prospects* want to happen.

Probing Gives You More Selling Power

The Probe step is the very core of the high impact selling system. When you probe, you look beneath the surface to discover and reveal what's really going on in the prospect's mind and heart.

The dictionary defines a probe as an instrument used to penetrate, usually for the purpose of measuring or investigating. As an action verb, *to probe* means to interview, to ask questions and listen, to observe, to study, and so on.

Probing enables you to do two very important things:

First, it enables you to discover what the prospect wants and the conditions under which the person will buy what you're selling. It keeps you from wasting a lot of time on prospects who won't buy what you're selling under any conditions. But, more importantly, it enables you to discover needs you can meet and suggest ways to meet them.

Second, probing enables prospects to identify, clarify, and express their wants or needs. Many people have only a vague feeling that they want *something* but don't have the foggiest idea what it is. Others may have a deep desire they've never even admitted to themselves. Some may think they want one thing, when what they really want is something entirely different. Still others know exactly what they want but don't know how to go about getting it.

By skillfully and sensitively probing, you can take the guesswork out of selling—and buying. You can avoid the amateurish technique of holding up one product after another and asking, "Is this it?" You can become a highly respected professional who renders a valuable service to your clients, a service for which you can expect to be paid very well.

I. HOW TO LISTEN PEOPLE INTO BUYING

Get yourself a leather binder, a really nice one, that contains a legal pad. Treat it as if it were the most valuable piece of equipment you have, for it may very well prove to be just that.

Once you are ready to start the Probe step, open it up as the prospect watches, take out a pen, and say, "In order for me to be of service to you, do you mind if I ask you a few questions?"

Then *stop!* Don't say another word until the person gives you permission to ask those questions. We can't emphasize enough how important this waiting interval is; it really sets a pattern for everything that follows throughout the course of your sales interview.

Mastering the Master Keys

Your primary objective in the Probe step is to listen your prospect into buying.

The master keys to the Probe step are *asking* and *listening*. They are your most effective implements for opening up the mind and heart of your prospect.

Unfortunately, many salespeople have great misconceptions about the meanings of those two key words, *asking* and *listening*. Let's look at what they've come to mean in typical sales jargon:

To *ask* means one thing—to ask for the order. In fact, asking people to sign an order blank is the first question some salespeople use. It's so common that most of us can't remember the last time a salesperson asked us a question such as, "How will you use it?" or "What do you like most about it?" Without these personal interest questions the buyer may well feel cheated.

To *listen,* means to be quiet while the prospect is talking so you can use the time to think up what you're going to say when he or she finishes.

High impact selling adopts totally different meanings for those two terms:

Asking means that if you ask enough of the right questions throughout the whole interview you'll more likely get an order.

Listening means that paying attention to what the prospect is saying is the most important task of the salesperson.

Later we'll explore how to use the master key of asking questions, but first let's examine two vital questions about listening:

1. Why do most salespeople find it so hard to really listen to what their prospects say?

2. How can you improve your listening skills?

Conditioned to Ignore the Prospect's Needs and Desires

What is uppermost in our minds as we walk into a prospect's turf? Don't be ashamed to say it: The number one thought in our mind is *to make a sale.* I think it's safe to say that most salespeople are primarily concerned about what they will get out of the sale—not what the prospect will get out of it.

The selfish streak in most of us has been given a big boost by much of the sales training we have received. In fact, the whole selling situation is geared toward satisfying our own needs and interests. We go out looking for "prospects" to buy what we're selling, try to warm them up so we can lay our pitch on them, then hit them with the close. If we do it well, we can make big money at it.

Now along comes Bill Brooks suggesting that we lay aside our own interests to discover and satisfy the needs and desires of our customers.

Self-Centeredness Is Not in Your Best Interest

Please don't get me wrong. I'm no martyr who lays himself at the feet of every client and cares nothing about his own needs.

What I'm suggesting to you is that there is a vast difference between self-centeredness and serving your own best interest. Let me express it in the following principle:

> Probe Principle # 1:
> The best way to serve your own interest
> is to put the needs and desires of your
> customer first!

If all you want to talk about is yourself—your interests, your products, your product's features, your company, . . . —don't be surprised if you encounter strong sales resistance from the outset.

If instead you focus your attention on the prospect—the prospect's interests, the prospect's needs and desires, the prospect's values—you will notice a remarkable difference in that person's openness to you.

> Probe Principle # 2:
> To deliver value to the prospect, you must
> see yourself primarily as a value resource
> for the prospect!

What keeps you from becoming a vending machine is that you have an opportunity to meet the widely varied and specific needs of each customer you serve. The most helpful attitude a salesperson can have is to see himself or herself as a resource for meeting the needs and fulfilling the desires of customers.

If the primary focus of your sales approach is creating value for individuals you are meeting, you will not only become a high impact salesperson, you will become a very rich salesperson.

But there is something you must do before you can become a value resource for your customer:

> Probe Principle # 3:
> To be a value resource for the prospect,
> you must first discover what the prospect
> perceives as value!

If I may paraphase a familiar old saying, "Value is in the eye of the beholder." That a product comes in 47 colors might be of little value to a person who is color blind. Something that is light-weight and easy to carry might be a real turnoff to a weight lifter. And a "40 percent savings" on an artificial heart is sure to have little value to a patient who merely has a headache!

Your selling impact rises in direct proportion to your understanding of the value system of your prospect. That leads us to the second vital question we raised about listening.

How Can You Improve Your Listening Skills?

People who talk themselves out of sales do a vast majority of the talking and a minority of the listening. But people who use their brains instead of their mouths do a vast majority of the listening and a minority of the talking during the Probe step.

Listening is a skill that can be learned and can also be continuously improved, but most of us have never been trained to listen. For example, which do we do most during the day, read or listen? Most of us generally listen more than we read, yet how many listening skills have we been taught?

Here are some pointers that can help you sharpen your listening skills:

1. Open your mind and ears—be receptive to the messages the person is giving.

2. Start listening from the first word and give the person your undivided attention.

3. Focus on what is being said. Avoid trying to figure out what the person is going to say; you may miss what he or she actually says.

4. Don't try to read your own meanings into what you think the person is saying. Actively assist the other person in conveying his or her meanings accurately to you.

5. Never interrupt! It cuts off the flow of dialog. Besides, it's offensive and rude.

6. Use questions to encourage people to talk and to clarify your understanding of what they mean.

7. Make notes of important points. Look for connections between apparently isolated remarks.

8. Control outside interruptions and distractions.

9. Get your whole body involved in listening and show that you are paying attention. Look the person squarely in one eye, and use facial expressions and gestures to show that you hear and understand what's being said.

10. Stay cool! Don't overreact to highly charged words and tones. Hear the person out, then respond. Most people will cool down and begin to talk calmly once their anger and frustrations are vented.

Remember, your objective is to listen your prospect into buying, not merely to "get your two cents worth in."

II. HOW TO DISCOVER WHAT PEOPLE WILL BUY

Your second objective in the Probe step is to discover what they will buy, why they will buy it, and under what conditions they will buy it.

The master key for doing that is asking the right kinds of questions.

"Oh, I ask a lot of questions," a furniture salesman once told me confidently. Yet his sales manager had relayed to me that the man was working on his last chance because his sales had been so few and far between.

"What kinds of questions do you ask?" I probed.

"When people walk into the store, I usually ask, 'Can I help you?'," he said. "Usually, they want to look around a little, so I just back off.... When I see that they've found something they seem to like, I go right up and ask, 'Can I fix you up with that bedroom suite today?'"

After thinking about how many times I'd heard salespeople ask questions like that, I began to look for ways to introduce him to a much more effective line of questioning.

"What do you learn by asking 'Can I help you?'," I asked him.

"I learn whether they want to buy something, or if they are just looking around," he answered.

"How many people have told you they wanted to buy something when you asked them that opening question during the last week?" I pressed.

"Oh, let's see.... I think there have been two, but we didn't have what one of them was looking for," he said sadly.

Ask and Ye Shall Learn—If Ye Ask the Right Questions

Can you see how much more I learned by the two questions I asked him, than he learned by asking his two questions?

First, let's take a look at what he learned:

1. He learned his prospects could talk.
2. He learned they weren't going to take his furniture away from him.
3. He learned (by prematurely asking a bad close question) that they were not ready to make a buying decision.

Now, let's see what my questions revealed:

1. I learned that he was presenting himself as a servant instead of a skilled professional. "Can I help you?" is the kind of question people expect from the Salvation Army, not from a real sales professional!

2. I learned that his questions were setting up about a 99 percent chance for a negative response. Questions that call for a "yes" or "no" produce about ten times as many "no" responses as "yes" answers.

3. I learned that his line of questioning gained him no insights about *what* his prospects wanted—what they would buy, and what needs they were seeking to satisfy, or under what conditions they would buy.

4. I learned that he was trying to close before he sold anything. He was asking for a buying decision before he gave his prospects any reasons to buy.

The list of things I learned from my two questions could go on and on, but the main thing I learned was that he would soon be out of a job unless he learned how to ask the right questions.

Let me share with you some of the tips I gave that young man about how to ask the right kinds of questions during the Probe step.

Tips on How to Ask the Right Questions

1. *Prepare, in advance, the questions you will ask.*

Of course, every prospect is unique and every selling situation requires some variation, but certain basic questions which come up in every interview can be planned in advance. By carefully planning them, you can make sure you cover all bases and that your wording is precise.

There is one caution: Be careful not to phrase them so they sound canned.

2. *Ask open-ended and indirect questions.*

Closed questions that call for a "yes" or "no" answer tend to discourage people from talking, to give only limited information, and to set a negative tone.

During the Probe step, ask open-ended questions that require prospects to tell you how they feel, what they want, or what they think.

For example, the furniture salesman I mentioned earlier might have asked: "How would you describe your decorating motif?"

3. *Ask need-development questions.*

In the Probe step, you want to do more than get the prospect to talk—you want that prospect to tell you what he or she needs. Therefore, frame questions that will give you insights into how prospects perceive their needs.

Our furniture saleman might ask: "What kinds of entertaining do you enjoy?" or "What kinds of activities does your family enjoy doing in the den?"

4. *Ask questions that help you identify dominant needs.*

Usually there is one overriding need in the prospect's mind—a need you can pinpoint by asking the right questions.

"What do you like least about your present car?" a car salesperson could ask.

5. *Ask questions that help you pinpoint the dominant buying motivations.*

Buying motivations and needs are not always the same. Buying motivations have to do with desires, feelings, tastes, and so on. For example, I sell a lot of my professional speaking services over the phone. When a prospective client says that he or she is considering booking me, I will often ask: "Who have you had in the past?" Their answers will often reveal what kinds of speakers they like. If all they give me is a list of names, I at least learn what kinds of speeches they like. Often, however, they will talk about one or two who were particularly well received by their audiences, and why they were so popular. Then I know exactly what benefits to emphasize most.

You might discover the same sort of information by asking, "Who are you buying from now?"

6. *Avoid offensive questions or asking questions in an insensitive way.*

Some questions can offend prospects and cause them to back up from you. Some examples of pitfalls to avoid are:

- Don't use leading or "setup" questions such as, "You do want your children to have a fair chance, don't you?" What is the prospect going to say? "No! Let the little brats tough it out!"
- Nosey questions can be a real turnoff. Asking a woman, "What time will your husband be home?" might be asking her for information she doesn't wish to give out to strangers.
- Sometimes your manner can be threatening. Instead of asking, "How much can you afford to spend?", why not phrase it, "How much had you planned to invest?"

7. *Start with broad questions, then move toward questions with a narrower focus.*

Broad questions are usually less threatening and yield general information. Thus, they can help you get things rolling and steer you in the right direction. An example of a broad question might be: "What kind of look do you prefer in drapes?"

However, as your probing becomes more comfortable and picks up speed, you will need to get more specific with your questions.

"What size are the windows in your living room?" is a good example of a narrow question.

8. *Ask questions that are easy to answer.*

Questions that require knowledge the prospect doesn't have can often make a person feel stupid. For example, asking most consumers, "What's the maximum wattage per channel on your amplifier?" might get you a dumb look for an answer. The smarter you make your prospects feel, the smarter they'll think you are and the better they'll like you.

9. *Use questions to guide the interview and keep it positive in tone.*

Some people love to ramble on and on, but by skillfully using questions you can keep the interview focused and moving in the right direction. It is always a good idea to avoid explosive subjects like religion, politics, race, and deep personal problems.

Also, ask questions to which people can easily respond in a positive manner. Studies have shown that most people much prefer to agree than to assert themselves and disagree. Make it easy to say "yes."

10. *Ask—then shut up and listen.*

The prospect can't talk while you're talking. Besides, you can't learn while you're talking. Don't just get quiet and think up something to say next; listen to and analyze every word that prospect says.

Remember: You can't talk people into buying, but you can listen them into it. Questions are your greatest selling tool. The better you become at asking questions, the easier it will become for you to sell.

III. HOW TO HELP PEOPLE CLARIFY FOR THEMSELVES WHAT THEY NEED AND WANT

The third major objective in the Probe step is to enable prospects to admit to themselves their own needs or desires.

Remember, a buying decision is ultimately an emotional response. It can be either reinforced or cancelled out by the way you present facts and focus relative values.

Let me give you a typical example of how it all too often works. A couple walks into a store and begins looking at a product, say, a reclining chair.

"Can I fix you up with that new recliner today?" the salesperson asks.

"No thanks! We're just looking," comes the cool reply.

The salesperson quickly sizes the prospects up and decides they're a time waster, and goes back to something important like shooting the bull with other salespeople.

That's not selling—it's peddling!

First, that salesperson jumped right over the meeting, probing, applying, and convincing steps and tried to close the sale. He or she tried to collect money without giving any value.

Second, the salesperson misread the most obvious signal any prospect can send out—walking into a store and looking over a piece of merchandise. You don't have to be very bright to figure out that these persons had some desire for a recliner.

Of course, a given prospect may have only a faint desire for a product, or the person may not have the resources to satisfy that desire. Then, too, your prospect may be nothing more than a lonely person who wants to talk to someone. But you won't know unless you take the time to find out.

Third, the salesperson did nothing to focus or reinforce the desire in the prospects' mind.

My purpose here is not to criticize salespeople. The fact is that during talks with thousands of salespeople who've attended my seminars, I've discovered that most of them simply don't know how to help their prospects clarify their own feelings and desires. That's why I've chosen to close out this chapter with some tested and proven pointers on how to do just that.

Pointer # 1:
Seek to Understand the Prospect's
Deepest Feelings

A prospect is not an adversary; however, some of the things a prospect feels or thinks can, at the very least, be a hindrance, if not an enemy, to your closing the sale.

For example, confusion, misinformation, false conclusions, and negative feelings can all work against you in your efforts to close a sale. Unless you understand what a prospect is thinking and feeling, you are at a distinct disadvantage. That's one reason it is so important to be a good listener.

However, selling also involves the art of being alert, perceptive, and creative in searching out what your prospects really feel or think about their own needs and desires. Let me illustrate this by relating a true story about one of my sharpest acquaintances in real estate.

A man and his wife came to her in response to an ad for a house she had listed. The woman did all the talking at first and was enthusiastic about everything the salesperson told her about the house. However, the man started finding fault with the house the moment they drove up. The woman loved it, but the man rejected it outright.

After the same thing happened at two more houses, the salesperson sensed what was going on and began to probe more deeply into the man's unexpressed feelings. She found that the man felt the couple could not afford the houses they were looking at but didn't want to admit it to his wife. So his game was to find something wrong with every one of them.

The salesperson soon realized she could show them a dozen houses in the price range the wife wanted to see and still not close the sale. Tactfully, she steered them to a house the man felt they could afford.

Upon seeing a house he felt was in his budget range, the man quickly became the ally of the salesperson and began talking about all "the great possibilities" he saw for the house. The wife gave up some of her demands, and the sale was closed.

Sometimes there is a conflict of values between multiple parties who have to agree before a deal is made. More often, that conflict exists within almost every prospect we see. The better you become at spotting those internal conflicts, the more you can help your prospects work through them—and the more sales you can close.

Pointer # 2:
Assure Prospects You Want to Help Them
Meet Their Needs

Scientific studies have repeatedly shown that most people approach almost any buying decision with some anxiety, and often they have very mixed emotions.

For example, a prospect whose opening question is, "How much is it?" is very often looking for an excuse not to satisfy a need or desire he or she feels.

As a knowledgeable and skilled professional, you can often help such persons sort through their confusion and anxieties. In fact, many prospects regularly look to salespeople to help them make up their minds.

To recap, begin the Probe step by inviting the prospect to consider: "In order for me to be of service to you, do you mind if I ask you a few questions?" Then ask questions to determine how you can be of service, and end by assuring the client(s) that you want to help them meet their needs. In this way you have laid a solid foundation to proceed with the sales interview.

Pointer # 3:
Ask Questions to Focus Issues

If you feel, however, that certain issues are still hanging, it is important to clear them away before you move on to the Apply step. This is where salespeople who rely upon their jawbones rather than their "think-tanks" often make a big mistake. They give their own opinions to try to settle issues that linger in the prospect's mind.

For example, the salesperson who answers, "You can never have too much life insurance!" when the prospect says he's already overinsured is delaying dealing with a crucial issue—an issue that must be settled before a sale can be made. Perhaps even worse, the salesperson may be setting up a war of the wills she is bound to lose.

The high impact selling approach is to *ask questions* instead of making statements or giving opinions.

"May I ask why you feel you already have too much life insurance?" enables the prospect to examine what he's really feeling.

"Because I'm already spending a fortune on payments!" he may answer. That opens the way for a reflective question such as, "So you do agree that providing adequately for your family's security needs is a priority?"

Perhaps the best tactic for focusing a prospect's needs and feelings is to keep weighing one value against another. You might use questions to contrast "a little sacrifice now" with "the peace of mind that comes from knowing your son's education will be provided for if, for some unforeseen reason, you are not around to provide for it."

That brings me to another vital principle of the probe step:

Probe Principle # 4:
All values are considered equal in the
absence of a values interpreter.

What that means to you is that, as a professional, one of your key roles is to focus and interpret relative values for your prospects. If you do it well, they will very often reward you by becoming your happy clients.

TO SUM IT ALL UP...

The Probe step is the very core of the high impact selling system. It enables you to accomplish three important objectives:

1. "Listen" people into buying instead of talking your way out of the sale
2. Discover what they will buy, why they will buy it, and under what conditions they will buy it
3. Enable them to focus their needs and wants in their own minds

The better you become at asking questions and actively listening, the more often you can accomplish those three vital objectives. It's the kind of approach that separates the pros from the amateurs in selling.

ACTION STEPS

Mentally reconstruct a recent sales call in which you felt you could have closed the sale but failed to get the prospect's name on the dotted line. Ask yourself if one of the following happened:

1. Did you talk yourself out of the sale rather than listening the person into buying?

2. Did you fail to find out what the prospect would buy, or under what conditions he or she would buy?

3. Did you fail to help the prospect focus his or her own needs and wants?

CHAPTER 7

Step Four: Apply

How to Show People You Can Meet Their Greatest Need

PURPOSE

Demonstrating your product is essentially a process of applying what you sell to the needs and wants of your prospects. In this chapter, you'll discover how to:

1. Show and tell with the power to sell
2. Answer the prospect's biggest question to get the action you want
3. Build more value for added sales punch
4. Target the "hot button" to heighten desire
5. Ask for prospects' reactions and feelings about what they have seen and heard

> *To a prospect, any price is*
> *too high until he or she*
> *understands the value of*
> *a product or service.*

TO PUT MORE POWER IN YOUR DEMONSTRATION, THINK APPLICATION

I've chosen to call this the Application step rather than the Demonstration step for one big reason—it describes more accurately what needs to happen for you to consistently make sales.

In sales jargon, *to demonstrate* has come to mean to show how something works, what it looks like, and all it will do. As hard as it may be to believe, hard facts are relatively minor considerations to most consumers. On the contrary, overloading a prospect with too many data can work against you in making a sale. However, *to apply* suggests that you show prospects how they can get what they want most by buying what you are selling.

Let me tell you a story to illustrate what I mean. An audiovisual studio in my area was struggling against tremendous apathy in trying to sell its services. The sales department had put together some multimedia presentations that would knock your eyes out. Their soundtracks were powerful and effective. Yet nobody seemed interested in buying multimedia presentations and dramatic soundtracks—especially not at the prices they charged. They even tried cutting their prices, offering special deals, and throwing in bonuses. But none of these tactics worked either.

Finally, the company's chief salesman got a brilliant idea. The studio put together a sample product training film that could be used by furniture reps to train retail floor salespeople in how to sell their company's products. He took the sample to a large furniture manufacturer and explained how the company's reps could increase their sales by helping retailers move more of their furniture.

Bingo! The manufacturer was thrilled! The firm immediately bought a projector for each of its 270 salespeople, ordered several product training films, and contracted with the studio to teach their salespeople how to use them in training. Soon other firms got in on the action, and within a year the struggling multimedia studio was expanding like crazy.

What made the difference? The sales team quit demonstrating their impressive presentations and started applying what they could do to meet their prospects' needs.

Discovering How to Apply

Of course, the idea of applying what you sell to what your prospect wants and needs most is not new. Actually, many sales trainers spend a great deal of time telling people they "ought to do it," but they never say how.

In this chapter, we want to move beyond the "ought to's" and focus on exactly how you can do it. Let's begin with "how to" number one.

I. HOW TO SHOW AND TELL WITH MORE POWER TO SELL

Whether what you know about your products and services will become an asset or a liability to you in selling depends upon one thing—how you use what you know.

For example, let's say you know absolutely nothing about personal computers, but you are exploring the possibility of buying one. You go into your friendly neighborhood computer store and start looking around. Typically, what will happen is that some computer jock will pounce upon you, "Can I fix you up with a PC today?"

"No, what I'd really like to see is a personal computer," you respond timidly. When you see the "Oh, brother!" look in his eye, it dawns on you that PC stands for personal computer.

"We're running a special on this model all this week and it's a real bargain," he volunteers. "It comes with 640K RAM, one floppy drive, and a built-in ten megabyte hard disk.... And you can also include a tape backup for about $800 extra. Is that going to be big enough for you, or do you need something larger?"

"Uhhh, I think that's plenty big," you stammer. "I don't have too much room on my desk."

He slowly shakes his head and points out that what he really asked was if it would provide enough capacity to meet your needs. You admit that you didn't even know that capacity was a factor, and that you have no idea how much of it you need.

What you'd really like for that salesperson to do would be to probe into your needs and wishes, right? Once he or she understood what you needed and wanted, you'd probably like for the person to recommend the system that would most adequately meet your needs at a price you could afford.

These are the kinds of services a truly professional salesperson seeks to develop—what we call putting more sell in your show and tell.

Pointer # 1:
Choose the Most Appropriate Product
or Service

As simple as it sounds, choosing the right product to show is a vital part of the Application step. Yet it is also one of the most troublesome. It is troublesome for two big reasons: *First,* salespeople often skip right over the Probe step and jump right into a demonstration. After all, they reason, there's no need to waste time. The prospect generally knows what he or she wants, and other products up or down the line can be shown later, right? Wrong!

For example, a photocopier salesman once confessed that he learned a valuable lesson by blowing a sale he could have made. A prospect's secretary called and said her boss wanted to see a copier that day, so the salesman set up an appointment for late that afternoon.

He threw the top-of-the line model into his station wagon and drove 50 miles to make the demo. He allowed plenty of time to set up because that baby could run colors, could collate thousands of pages, and could do everything but make coffee.

"I don't need all that stuff—we never do colors and we don't have any use for collating. What I want is a machine that will give me top quality prints of single pages and spit them out in a hurry," the prospect said as soon as he saw the machine. He didn't even ask the price.

When the salesman promised to be back the next morning with the right machine, the man said he was going out of town that night and suggested the salesman call for an appointment "next week." You can guess what happened next. When the salesman called back to make an appointment, he discovered that his prospect had bought a competitor's inferior product at a higher price than his deluxe job would have cost them.

Very often you get only one good shot at demonstrating your product or service. Anything you show after that is anticlimactic—

even if you get a second chance. Downgrading can be embarrassing for the client, and upgrading can be tough for you. The only way to be really sure what to show is to probe thoroughly until you are certain about your prospects' wants and needs.

Second, salespeople often show the wrong product because they choose what to show based on their own interests, not on the prospect's desires.

One of the criticisms I have against sales contests is that they often encourage salespeople to show one product to all clients because that's what the company is pushing at the moment. Thus, salespeople walk out with no order rather than an order for something that doesn't gain them a lot of points.

Smart professional salespeople know that the right choice of product or service to show is always the one that the prospect is most likely to buy.

Pointer # 2:
Tailor the Presentation to the Prospect's
Needs and Wants

Have you ever noticed how television producers use cameras to call your attention to what they want to emphasize? They'll give you a broad shot of a huge crowd of people, then they'll keep narrowing the field of vision by moving in closer. Eventually, they will focus on one person, even zooming in to capture facial expressions.

What they are doing is calling your attention to what they believe to be the focal point.

When it comes to demonstrating your products, there are four possible focal points:

1. You can focus on the product itself, which is what most salespeople do. They love to talk about all the gadgets, the features, and variations of their product.

2. You can focus on the company you represent and talk about their reputation for service, dependability, and fair prices.

3. You can focus attention upon yourself by noting that if you sell 200 widgets this week, you'll win a free trip to Bermuda, or by leveling with the prospect: "I want to tell you why I believe so strongly in this product."

4. You can focus on the prospect—what he or she wants or needs and what they will gain by ownership.

Let me tell you a little secret: Most prospects could not care less about the first three, but if you really hit on number four, you have a good chance of closing a sale. If you want to add more sell to your show and tell, get very personal with it.

Pointer # 3:
Give 'em a Show They'll Never Forget

Canned demonstrations are like a straightjacket—they limit your ability to tailor your presentation to the prospect's needs and desires. However, that does not mean that you need to go to the opposite extreme and slither through a completely spontaneous demonstration.

Actually, the application approach to demonstrating your product calls for harder work than a canned presentation. What it means is that you have to know everything about every product in your lineup—and you have to know it so well you can present it with equal enthusiasm and force in any sequence. That's a big order!

The most professional salespeople I know have so practiced demonstrating each feature and benefit they have to sell that they can present all their products with finesse and simplicity.

Pointer # 4:
Involve Your Prospect from the Word Go

A friend of mine told me he had decided to buy a certain expensive brand of automobile and went to a dealer's showroom to take a test drive.

"The salesman acted as if I were going to hurt his car," my friend recalled. "Every time I tried to touch anything on the instrument panel, he'd almost slap my hands. His attitude seemed to be, 'You do the paying, and leave the driving to us.'"

"Did you buy it!" I asked.

"Sure I bought a car just like the one I'd been shown, but not from him," he said wryly. "I went to another dealership and bought it from a salesman who put me in the driver's seat all the way."

Getting prospects involved in the process is a much more powerful way to help them experience the transfer of ownership, rather than relying on a contractual agreement to make the sale.

Real estate salespeople, for example, know that clients must experience psychological ownership of a property before they will sign a purchase agreement. Thus, they usually insist that the selling family not be at home when they show the property to a prospective buyer. They know that few families will come in and "take over" psychological ownership of a home from another family.

Some of the real pros I know in real estate actively try to get their prospects involved in planning what they will do to change the decor, and even where they will put their furniture. It helps them to see themselves actually living in the house.

This principle, which works in any selling situation, can be expressed in the following way:

> Applying Principle # 1:
> The transfer of ownership must occur in a
> prospect's mind before he or she will sign
> on the dotted line!

That mental transfer of ownership can only occur when you actively involve your prospects and enable them to see themselves using whatever you are selling. Selling is definitely a hands-on activity—especially when it comes to the prospect's hands.

II. HOW TO GET THE ACTION YOU WANT BY ANSWERING THE PROSPECT'S BIGGEST QUESTION

What would you say is ultimately the prospect's most important question?

"How much does it cost?" is the answer I usually get when I ask that question in one of my seminars.

But that answer is wrong! Although "How much does it cost?" is the most frequent question prospects ask, it is only a mask for the real question behind it.

The prospect's biggest question is always, "What's in it for me?" In other words, "What am I going to get for my money?"

When a prospect says, "It costs too much!", what he or she is really saying is, "It does not have more value to me than the money I would have to spend to get it."

Let me give you another very important principle:

> Applying Principle # 2:
> All sales degenerate into a struggle over price in the absence of a values interpreter!

If you satisfactorily answer the prospect's most important question—"What do I get for my money?"—price will be a minor consideration when you get ready to ask for the order.

Now if you are one of those salespeople who always seems to be haggling with customers over money, what I just said may sound too good to be true. I want to give you some tested and proven tips on how to avoid allowing price to become the major issue in a sales interview.

Tip # 1:
Avoid Making Price an Issue Yourself

Interestingly, studies show that the typical salesperson is a lot more concerned about price than is the typical customer.

Amateur salespeople seem to love to talk about price. They compare one product with another on the basis of costs; they talk incessantly about how big a discount they are able to give; and they boast about having a lower price than their competitors.

Unfortunately, all that does is serve to remind the prospect of how much the product is going to cost. Even if the prospect is not overly concerned about price at the beginning of the sales interview, he or she will become more and more attuned to it the more you talk about it.

The real pros at the selling game handle price as if it were a minor consideration. Of course, when the prospect makes it an issue, they deal with it effectively. But even then, they try to minimize its importance. The next three tips explain how professional salespersons minimize the cost factor.

Tip # 2:
Focus on Benefits—Not Features or Price

Do you understand the difference between a feature and a benefit? That may sound like an elementary question, but it focuses one of the most basic points of high impact selling.

A *feature* is a product or service attribute—something that is built into the product or service, or some quality that makes it attractive. A *benefit,* however, is an advantage that a particular feature provides. Benefits are what a given customer will derive from a particular feature.

For example, a handle on the top is a feature, but ease of handling is a benefit. Availability of service nationwide is a feature, but convenience to the customer is the benefit. An overdrive transmission is a feature, but better gas mileage is the benefit the customer will derive from ownership.

The best way to answer your prospect's most important question is to focus all your attention on what benefits the person will derive from using your product or service. This whole discussion may sound rather picayune, but the difference in impact is enormous. Let me explain further by commenting on the following principle:

Applying Principle # 3:
All values are considered equal until
someone points out the difference!

The smart salesperson never assumes that any fool can see that a handle on the top makes a product easier to carry—he or she shows *how much easier* it is to carry. In fact, really smart professionals will let the prospect *feel* how much easier it is to carry!

Never assume that a prospect understands the benefit a feature offers—always point it out. What's more, sell every benefit as if it were the greatest thing since sliced bread. The more benefits you apply to the prospect's needs or wants, the more often you show the prospect "what's in it for me."

Tip # 3:
Focus on Value and Work to Deliver It

Showing your prospect the benefits of ownership is the way you create value; in fact, it's the only way you have to create value. The more value you create, the more desirable the product or service becomes to the prospect, and the less important price becomes.

Sometimes I find it helpful to think of a sales interview as an old-fashioned set of balancing scales. On one side, the prospect puts all his or her negative feelings about what I'm selling, and I put all my benefits of ownership on the other side. When my values outweigh the prospect's negative feelings and objections, I've got myself a sale.

But I go beyond simply verbalizing those values, I work hard to make the prospect feel them. With a little ingenuity, I can usually get the prospect to feed back those values to me in his or her own words. Only then do I know for sure that they have accepted the values I have offered.

It works fantastically well!

Tip # 4:
Relate Every Benefit in Terms of a Value

One way you can focus attention on values is to relate every benefit in terms of a value.

The dictionary says that value is "worth in money" and that what gives something its value is its "desirability" to the person who values it. So your task is to translate every feature and benefit into a tangible value—something the prospect desires. Create enough desirability and you've got yourself a sale.

Many salespeople make a big deal of the difference between selling "tangible" and "intangible" values. A tangible value is one you can see, hear, touch, taste, or smell and is considered easier to sell. An intangible value has more to do with emotions, or logic, or some unseen factor.

My answer to that hassle over tangible and intangible values can be expressed in the following principle:

Applying Principle # 4:
All values are intangible until someone
makes them tangible, and all intangible
values can be made tangible with a
little creativity!

Travel agencies use vivid pictures of exotic places to make tangible for prospects the intangible value of getting away from it all. Whatever you are selling, every effort to translate benefits into tangible values your prospects can get their teeth into is worth its weight in gold.

That brings us to the next big way you can put more sell in your show and tell.

III. BUILD MORE VALUE FOR ADDED SALES PUNCH

Maybe it seems as if I'm talking a lot about value in this chapter on the Application step. If so, it's intentional. Building a sale is a little like building a house, and the building blocks are features and benefits translated into values for the prospect.

But there are some added considerations on the matter of building value. For example, when and how do you build value?

When to Build Added Value

Obviously, you build value every time you enable the prospect to connect with a benefit of ownership. But let's look at some other opportunities you have for building value:

First, build value every time the prospect expresses approval. If the prospect says, "Oh, I like that!" take advantage of the opportunity to talk about what a great value "that" is. Never brush aside such a comment but always seize it as a chance to let the prospect fall more deeply in love with whatever you are selling.

Second, build value as you answer each objection. Often an objection is nothing more than a request for more information or a greater reassurance of value. Keep in mind that objections don't just go away; they simply lie there like barriers you have to surmount to get your message across to the prospect. Face them forthrightly, and push them out of your way by adding values.

Third, build value each time the prospect asks a question. A question almost always is a request for a reason to buy—a value. Don't back away from it. Instead view it as an expression of interest and treat it as an invitation to pour on more value.

How to Build Added Value

Now let's look at some ways you can build value:

First, turn the prospect's questions and objections into questions. If the prospect asks, "How much does it cost?" ask, "How much had you planned to invest?" If the prospect says, "I can buy one a lot cheaper!" ask, "But can you get one you'd enjoy owning as much for less money?"

Second, summarize and review benefits frequently. What you know so well, your prospects don't know at all. You may be able to remember every minute feature and benefit you have covered, but don't expect that from the prospect. At best the average prospect will remember less than one out of five benefits you mention only once. However, people do learn by repetition, so keep reviewing all the benefits you cover—especially those the prospect seems to like most.

Third, keep focusing relative values. Remember, one of your most vital tasks in selling is to be a values interpreter. That suggests two important techniques:

1. A values interpreter relates each value to the prospect's needs and wants. The most fruitful sentence in the salesperson's vocabulary is, "What you get out of it, Mr. Smith, is . . . ."

2. A values interpreter constantly weighs one value against others. For example, if you're selling tires and a prospect says, "I like a wider stripe than that!" you might say, "I'm sure looks are important to you but don't you agree that your family's safety is what really matters?"

Always bear in mind that the more value you build, the greater your chances of making a sale.

Fourth, keep emphasizing the values that most directly satisfy the prospect's most compelling need. If you've done a good job of probing, you're aware of that one need the prospect feels is more pressing than all the others. Focus on those values that satisfy that need and keep hammering away at them until the prospect feels satisfied that buying what you are selling is the best way he or she can have that need met.

Going back to the balancing scales analogy, I've noticed that the fastest way to tip the scales on the value side is to pile in more and more values that relate directly to the prospect's most compelling need. In fact, a value that satisfies a client's most compelling need is worth at least ten values that matter only marginally to that person.

Now let's take a look at another way you can boost your customer impact by applying instead of just demonstrating.

IV. TARGET THE "HOT BUTTON" TO HEIGHTEN DESIRE

One of the all-time classic stories of "hot button" selling is one in which the principal characters are a real estate salesman, a woman, and a cherry tree in full blossom.

"Oh! Look at that cherry tree... I've never seen so many blossoms!" the woman shouted as they drove up to look at a house.

"Do you like cherry blossoms?" the cagey salesman asked. Any fool could see the answer to that one, but he wanted her to tell him how much she liked them.

"I've always wanted a cherry tree in my yard!" she said.

"The yard's too small!" her husband quickly grunted.

Guess where that salesman took them first. You guessed it— right to the back yard to look at that tree! He even picked a blossom and gave it to her.

"The patio door needs to be replaced," noted the husband once they were in the dining room.

"Yes, but look at the view of that cherry tree!" said the salesman.

"The kitchen window is mighty small," said the woman.

"It is small, but you can see that cherry tree while you're washing dishes," the guy said.

"This is a crazy shape for a master bedroom," complained the man when they went upstairs.

"Wow! You can smell those blossoms from here!" the salesman said as he threw open a window.

To make a long story short, he sold the cherry tree to that couple for $50,000, and threw in the house as a bonus.

That's what targeting the "hot button" is all about. It's finding that one benefit the prospect gets most excited about and constantly bringing everything back to it—a powerful sales technique.

How to Find the "Hot Button"

Granted, it is not always easy to find what turns the prospect on about your product or service. In fact, many prospects are so guarded in their reactions that they will deliberately try to conceal any warm feelings they have about any benefit. That's especially true of professional buyers.

Yet despite the difficulty in finding the "hot button" sometimes, it is very important to keep trying. Here are some suggestions that can help you spot the key benefit for your prospect:

First, stay alert for it during the Probe step. For example, if prospects say they need a station wagon to haul their four kids around, ask, "Would you say having plenty of room for your children is the biggest reason you want to trade cars?" If the answer is "yes," make a note of it, show them the biggest station wagon on your lot, and ask, "Don't you agree that this one has plenty of room for your family?" Let the kids ride in the back if they are with their parents. If not, you ride in the back to emphasize the roominess.

Second, look and listen for the slightest clue to a "hot button" response. It may show up in the way the prospect caresses the texture of a product, or the client may keep coming back to some feature or ask a lot of questions about something you have mentioned. For example, a prospect may tell you he's looking for a cheap television set, but if he keeps wandering off to a giant screen model, at least explore what that means. Professional selling requires total concentration.

Third, if you don't know, ask. That's right; just come right out and ask, "What do you like most about what I've shown you?" Once you ask, get real quiet, listen, and watch carefully. Nine times out of ten you'll find out exactly what you ask.

Whatever method you use to find the prospect's "hot button," zero in on that dominant benefit and use it as the foundation for everything that follows in making the sale.

V. ASK FOR A PROSPECT'S FEELINGS AND REACTIONS

The last stage of the Apply step is to ask prospects to share openly with you how they feel about what they've seen and heard. That idea scares high-pressure salespeople to death. They'd rather assume they're making the sale until the prospect beats them over the head and runs them out. But there's no need to fear asking the prospect such a question—particularly if you've been asking questions right along.

Asking for the prospect's reactions and feelings does three very important things for you:

First, it lets you know where you stand. You might discover that you can close the sale if you can clear up one or two issues. You might also discover that there are several conditions to be met before you can wrap it up. Or you might discover that you can't make the sale under any conditions. At least you'll know what you need to do—even if it's to pack up and move on.

Second, by asking, you enable prospects to admit to themselves how they feel and commit to you on how they'll act. By verbalizing their feelings, they can often clarify things in their own minds. You'll probably have smoother sailing once your clients can hear their own voices saying, "I like it!"

Third, it enables you to reinforce positive feelings and clear up any misconceptions prospects may have. By getting their reactions, you can test to see if you have communicated what you had intended. If they understand what you've said and feel positive about it, you can reinforce the values you've created and help them move toward psychological ownership. On the other hand, you might discover they have misunderstood some point you have made. If so, you can clear it up before you move on.

TO SUM IT ALL UP...

In this chapter, we have seen that to sell you have to do more than merely demonstrate what you are selling—you have to apply the most appropriate product or service to the needs and wants you discovered during the Probe step.

To do that, you will need to

1. Show and tell with the power to sell
2. Answer the prospect's biggest question
3. Build more value for added sales punch
4. Target the "hot button" to heighten desire
5. Ask for prospects' reactions and feelings about what they have seen and heard

Next, we'll see how important it is to convince your prospect of the validity of every claim you have made.

ACTION STEPS

Review your sales presentation to see how you might put more power in it by using the following suggestions:

1. Thinking application instead of features
2. Answering the *What's in it for me?* question for your prospects
3. Building more value by tuning in to your prospects' needs/desires
4. Targeting the prospect's "hot button"
5. Talking openly with your clients about their feelings and reactions to what you've shown them

CHAPTER 8

Step Five: Convince

How to Make People Believe Enough to Act

PURPOSE

In the Convince step, your task is to back up all the claims you have made about your product or service—in short to make your clients believe enough to act on your business proposal. In this chapter you'll discover how to do that by:

1. Proving your claims
2. Bringing your own witnesses
3. Justifying your price
4. Relieving the fear of buying

> *A truth ignored*
> *is no better than*
> *a lie accepted.*

YOU'VE GOTTA' MAKE 'EM BELIEVE

A recent Gallup poll showed that salespeople rank among the lowest of all professionals in credibility.

There's an old joke that asks, "Do you know how you can always tell when a salesman is lying?"

"No!" comes the reply.

"If he waves both arms in the air, he may be telling you the truth.... If he jumps all over the place and won't look you in the eye, he still may be telling you the truth.... But if he ever opens his mouth, he's lying!"

How deserved the reputation for dishonesty among salespeople may be is a matter of opinion, but the important fact we all have to face is that it is real. What makes it such a crucial fact is that our livelihood depends upon how much people believe what we say.

A second important piece of reality is that each prospect has his or her own valuing system against which all other values are measured. Prospects will do what they want to do, or at least what they believe is best for them.

The challenge can be stated as a principle:

> Convince Principle # 1:
> What people believe strongly enough,
> they act upon!

If people believe strongly enough that what you are selling will be worth more to them than the money you're asking for it, they'll buy it. If they don't, they won't! It's that simple.

If you are going to make a good living at selling, your only choice is to find ways to cut through all the mistrust and conflicting values to convince your prospects (1) that what you say is true and (2) that the benefits you offer outweigh the price you are asking.

That's a big order, but thousands of truly professional salespeople do it every day, and you can, too. In this chapter, we'll look at exactly how you can *consistently* convince prospects of the value of your product or service—time after time, day after day.

There are basically four actions you can take to convince your prospects and set the stage for them to buy:

1. Prove your claims
2. Bring your own witnesses
3. Justify your price
4. Relieve the prospect's fear of buying

Let's explore them one at a time.

I. PROVE YOUR CLAIMS

It might damage your ego, but it will certainly help your bank account to assume that most prospects will not believe anything you say unless you prove it to them. In all fairness, we must admit that most of our prospects have a right to be skeptical about our claims for several reasons:

First, we stand to gain something if they believe us. Former Secretary of State Henry Kissinger recently told about a reaction he once got from the late Chairman Mao Tse-tung of China.

"What do you want from us?" Chairman Mao asked bluntly.

"We don't want anything but your friendship," Mr. Kissinger replied.

"If you want nothing, you shouldn't be here; and if I wanted nothing, I wouldn't have invited you here," said the crafty old chairman.

Today's alert shoppers feel the same way. They know that you stand to gain something if they buy, so they balance everything you say against that fact.

Second, they've been lied to before. The Federal Trade Commission's "truth in advertising" rules have made it harder to get away with lying, but a person who wants badly enough to get around them can stretch the truth enough that it is essentially a lie. If you doubt that, all you have to do is think about your own experiences in buying.

Third, people have become jaded by oversell. By the time the average person in this country reaches adulthood, he or she will have seen more than a million television commercials (and heard nearly as many radio spots) promising everything from robust health and instant wealth to perpetual happiness. To survive, most people have developed very effective mental tune-out devices that just filter out any promise they question.

For example, I heard about a salesman whose son once asked, "Dad, are you telling me the truth or is that just sales talk?"

These and other factors make the Convince step absolutely crucial to your selling success. You have to prove every claim you make about your product or service, about your company, and about yourself.

Here are some ways you can do it.

Claim Prover # 1:
Never Make a Claim You Can't Back up
with Facts

In the first chapter of this book, I suggested that personal and professional integrity are absolutely essential to successful selling in today's marketplace. I want to reemphasize at this point how vital honesty is and to suggest that making false claims will cost you more sales than it will gain for you.

But there is another issue that is equally important. It is not enough for you to believe that a claim is true; you must be able to back it up with proof the prospect will accept.

Let me give you a principle that can help you enormously in building credibility:

> Convince Principle # 2:
> It makes little difference what you
> believe is true, unless you can prove it
> to your prospect.

My experience has shown me that one claim proved is worth 100 claims only made, and one false claim discovered can do more damage than a truckload of claims proved.

Claim Prover # 2:
If You Can Prove It, Show Your Evidence

It is important that you actively back up every claim you make, especially those that sound too good to be true.

The smart salesperson frequently offers supporting data, validating documents, and tangible evidence to prove every claim he or she makes. Obviously, not every prospect will doubt every claim you make, unless you look like Al Capone. But, since you can never really know which prospects will doubt which claims, the safest route is to prove them all.

Here are a couple of pointers to keep in mind:

First, the more dramatic and outstanding the claim, the more proof it usually requires. If you claim your gadget can triple a person's gas mileage, you'd better plan to show a lot of evidence to back it up.

Second, constantly test to make sure you've given enough evidence for each claim. For example, if a prospect says, "Oh, I know that's true!", it's safe to move on to the next point.

Claim Prover # 3:
Reinforce All Claims Visually

"A picture is worth a thousand words," the ancient Orientals used to say. The reason most people believe that statement, however, is that it has proven true in their own experience. What that means to you is that prospects will much more easily believe and remember what you *show* them than what you only *tell* them.

Simple graphic proof serves to (1) speed up your proof, (2) make your claim easier to grasp and believe, and (3) enable your prospects to remember it longer.

Claim Prover # 4:
Let Prospects Experience It Themselves

"The proof of the pudding is in the eating" is a time-proven adage. If you claim that your product is easy to carry, let the person pick it up and carry it around. If you claim your product is simple and easy to use, let clients see for themselves just how simple and easy it is.

This can be a tough assignment with some products or services (such as life insurance) and with some types of selling (like selling by telephone). That's one reason so many companies make "free trial offers." However, no matter how tough it is, every bit of creative effort you put into helping people experience for themselves the claims you make will be richly rewarded by increased credibility.

Claim Prover # 5:
Repeat Important Claims and Proofs
Again and Again

Have you ever wondered why major companies keep repeating the *same* commercials over and over? A logical answer might be that they cost so much to produce. However, a typical company will spend more money on air time to run a commercial just once than it spends on actual production.

The reason companies keep repeating the same commercials over and over ad infinitum (sometimes ad nauseum) is that studies show it is the best way to get people to believe them, remember them, and act upon them.

When you are selling, the more often you repeat something, the better your chances of having it accepted and remembered. That brings us to the second big task you have in the Convince step.

II. BRING YOUR OWN WITNESSES

What do the courts view as the strongest evidence in a trial? You guessed it—an eyewitness! What is the strongest theme in advertising? Word of mouth! Likewise, what's the most convincing evidence you can use to prove your claims for your product or service? An endorsement from a satisfied customer!

Here's a principle that explains why an endorsement is such powerful evidence that your product and service claims are true:

> Convince Principle # 3:
> Prospects expect salespeople to make
> claims for what they are selling, but they
> are impressed when someone else makes
> or endorses those claims.

An important corollary of this principle is never to make a claim for yourself or your product that you can get someone else to make for you.

Now let's take a look at how you can use the powerful technique of bringing your own witnesses to effectively boost your sales.

Witness Pointer # 1:
Try to Get a Written Endorsement from
Every Customer

The best way to get endorsements is to ask for them—it's that simple! Yet you'd be surprised at how many salespeople either neglect it or are afraid to do it.

What I usually do is to explain to customers that their name is widely respected and that I would appreciate an opportunity to mention them as a satisfied customer. At that point, many of them will volunteer to write a letter for me. If they agree for me to use their name but don't volunteer to write a letter, I come right out and ask for one. Only a very few will turn me down, and then it's for personal or professional reasons. Most people feel flattered that I think a letter from them will matter that much.

To make sure I get the promised letter, I will often suggest coming by a few days later to pick it up and thus saving them the trouble of mailing it. When I go back, I always try to see the customer and thank him or her personally. Interestingly, you'd be surprised how many leads I pick up on those second trips around.

One caution: Make sure your satisfied customers understand that you plan to use their letter as a promotional device. If you don't and they later find out you've used it, it can cause a misunderstanding.

Witness Pointer # 2:
Select Carefully the Endorsements
You Use with Each Prospect

Let's face it; we are all imitators. We imitate the people we respect and admire, and sometimes those we wish to impress. It's one of the strongest buying motivations.

Many of my car dealer clients have made a very interesting discovery by asking people a few questions when they buy a new car. One of the most frequent reasons people give for buying a new car goes something like this: "My neighbor (or co-worker or friend) bought a new car, and I started thinking maybe it was time I looked into it."

Haven't you tried out a new restaurant or store or product because a friend said he or she liked it? Of course you have and so have I!

The more recognizable a name is, the more convincing it will be to your prospect. That's one good reason to find out during the

Investigating and Probing steps all you can about every prospect you call upon. If you can show a prospect an endorsement from a golfing or bridge partner, a business associate, or a personal friend, it's like money in the bank.

If you can't find an endorsement from someone the prospect knows, you might choose endorsements from people of similar ages, with similar interests, and similar social status.

Witness Pointer # 3:
Treat Endorsements with Dignity
and Respect

An endorsement letter is worth many times its weight in pure gold—so treat it with dignity and respect. That suggests several things:

First, only speak of your customers as if you think they are the greatest people in the world. They are!

Second, protect your endorsements. I would suggest you put them in plastic sleeves to keep them looking fresh and new.

Third, show them as if you feel you are granting the prospect a special privilege to see them. If, for example, you rapidly flip them across a table at a prospect, you create several problems:

1. You don't give your client time to read them, so it appears as if you are hiding something.
2. Your behavior is contemptuous of both the client and the folks who gave you an endorsement.
3. You make the prospect hesitant to give you an endorsement. Who wants to be included in an arsenal of missiles you toss across tables at people?

People who give you endorsements show a great deal of trust, and prospects watch the respect you give your customers. So treat them with dignity and respect.

Witness Pointer # 4:
Try to Involve Happy Customers
with Prospects

Sometimes you can get a prospect to make an appointment for you with a friend, neighbor, or associate. If you can, it's a most convincing piece of evidence.

What I'm talking about is vastly different from the old high-pressure tactic of giving people a discount or premium for furnishing you with leads or actually setting up appointments for you. Most people react very negatively to that sort of tactic.

Let me explain what I'm talking about by using the case of a furniture rep who works out of my area. This guy has set up a mutual sharing network among the dealers who buy from him. When a furniture retailer gets a big response from an ad or sale on his products, the salesman will ask for permission to share that ad with other retailers in his territory but not in the same town. Since the salesman often shares winning ads and sales from other stores with him, he's usually glad to cooperate.

The salesman then takes that ad to other stores and suggests they run a similar sale—featuring his products, of course. "If you have any question about how well the ad works, call Joe at Smith's Furniture and ask him," he'll say. Sometimes he even suggests they call him "right now." If they call, Joe is proud of his idea and sells the prospect on it, the prospect is happy to find something that will sell furniture for him, and the salesman writes up a big order. That salesman has sold as much as five boxcar loads of furniture in one week, on one ad.

It takes a lot of creativity and some finesse to pull it off, but it is incredibly convincing. Why not look for some ways you can get your satisfied customers involved in selling for you?

Now let's look at the third big task in the Prove step.

III. JUSTIFY YOUR PRICE BY PROVING VALUE

Before prospects will buy what you're selling, you have to prove it is worth more to them than the actual dollar cost. But before you can do that, you have to believe it yourself. If you don't sincerely feel your product or service is a bargain to your customers, you'll have a tough time justifying the price you are charging. What's more, if you are just trying to sell something to make a quick buck, you'll find it a hard way to make a living.

I've already said so much about believing in what you're selling that I will merely restate the question: Do you believe that what you are selling represents a real value to your customers? If you don't, you owe it to yourself and everyone else to either convince yourself or quit selling it.

Appealing to a Jury of One

Aside from you, the only person whose opinion really matters is the prospect to whom you are selling. If that person believes he or she can get enough value to justify the cost, you've got a sale; if not, you haven't. It's that simple!

But, as we have seen, what is simple is not always easy. Let's explore some ways you can justify your price in the prospect's mind.

Price Justifier # 1: The Value Meter

A value meter is an imaginary device you create in the prospect's mind to indicate just how much value you have created for him or her. If you like, you can even illustrate this graphically by a visual meter which you move up every time you add another new value. However you do it, it is vital that you make the prospect keenly aware of how much value he or she will receive for the money spent.

Many salespeople do it by frequently conducting a values review. They may not call it that, but they keep summarizing all the values they've demonstrated.

I'm sure you've seen a rather "hokey" version of it in some television commercials selling overpriced merchandise at a bargain. The announcer will say, "You get this complete 12-piece set of super-sharp knives, plus this handy butcher's guide, plus this European chef's cookbook, plus the Brooklyn Bridge . . . all for the unbelievably low price of $19.95 . . . . That's a whopping $3 million value, and it's all yours for this special TV-offer price of $19.95 . . . . "

The TV hucksters' application may be very bad, but their basic idea is very good. In fact, it's one of the most effective techniques for justifying your price. You simply stack up the values in the mind of the prospect until they are convinced your price is reasonable.

Sell every benefit as if it were the greatest of all values, and just keep adding more of them.

Price Justifier # 2: Personalize All Values

The most significant question you must help your prospect answer will be "Is this worth what it will cost me?"

It may help to know that *Consumer's Guide* rates it as a good value, or that it is "widely acclaimed" by experts as the best bargain in its field; but the ultimate test will always be, "Is it worth it to me?"

That's why probing is so vital to the whole high impact selling system. It's where you find out what personal values matter enough to your prospect to justify whatever you will charge for your product or service. Once you become acquainted with a person's priorities, you can offer benefits to satisfy them. If you offer enough benefits, and benefits that are tailored to meet personal desires/interests, you can convince a person that your price is not too high.

For example, many of my clients sell automobiles that cost in excess of $20,000. Now, mere transportation might not be worth that price to most people, but prestige, comfort, reliability, styling, or luxury—or a combination of those values—might tip the scales to justify the price in the prospect's mind.

But remember, the more personal the benefits, and the higher they rank in the prospect's value system, the greater will be their value in justifying the price.

Price Justifier # 3: Interpret Relative Values

As we have seen, all values are considered equal until someone points out the difference.

For example, a friend of mine sells rather sophisticated home security systems that may carry pricetags of over $10,000.

"It's not worth that to me," a man may say when he is finally quoted a price.

That's when my friend becomes a values interpreter. He will turn to the man's wife and say something like this: "Mrs. Brown, your husband has told me he travels a great deal, right? Would it be worth that much money to you to know that you are safe from possible intruders, and that you can sleep comfortably when your husband is not here to protect you?"

"It sure is!" she will usually say.

"Uhhh! Where do I sign?" the man then asks.

Suddenly a different interpretation of values has raised significantly the value of the product.

When someone says, "Your price is too high," start asking yourself "Compared to what?" Compared to peace of mind? Compared to being the best dressed person you know? Compared to convenience? Compared to an inferior product? Compared to what?

Once you have found the value (or combination of values) the prospect considers higher than the price, interpret that as a benefit to the prospect.

Price Justifier # 4: Sell the Key Benefit

Remember the "hot button"? It's your greatest justification for the price your prospect must pay to get whatever you are selling.

Advertising agencies often ask their clients, "What is your unique selling proposition?" In other words, what is there about your product or service that sets it apart as being superior to all other products or services on the market.

When it comes to selling, the answer to that question is always "the benefit this prospect finds most attractive." To the real estate salesman in the previous chapter, it was a cherry tree in the backyard. It may be a certain look, a convenience, a texture or feel, a sense of security, or anything else the prospect falls in love with.

Whatever it is, it's the key benefit because it's the one which will open the door to the sale. The greatest justification for paying any price is, "I like it!" Your task is to help that prospect like what you are selling enough to pay the price for it.

Now let's look the one remaining task left in the Convincing step.

IV. RELIEVE THE PROSPECT'S FEAR OF BUYING

Fear can be one of the strongest motivations a prospect may have for buying a product or service, but it can also be one of the greatest deterrents to deciding positively.

In fact, fear of buying often proves to be one of the toughest challenges a salesperson faces. It may grow out of the person's fear of failure, fear of poverty, fear of ridicule or rejection, fear of the unknown, and so on ad infinitum.

Your task is to assist prospects in overcoming enough of whatever fear they feel to make them comfortable enough to buy. How can you do that?

First, we'll look at an important principle of convincing your prospect; then we'll explore some techniques you can use to make it work for you.

Convince Principle # 4:
As trust in you and confidence in the value
you are offering rises, fear of buying
disappears.

The greatest fear busters are trust and value. Let's look at some ways you can make them work for you as you seek to convince your prospects to buy.

Buying Fear Reliever # 1:
Reconcile the Buying Decision with
Their Value System

Any time we set out to act in a manner that is inconsistent with the way we see ourselves, we can expect to feel some fear. That's true even if what we are doing is a very good thing.

For example, many people who leave a "secure" job with a steady salary and set out to work in sales on straight commission are scared that they will fail and be humiliated. Years from now, they may look back on it as one of the greatest steps they ever took, but for the moment it is threatening to their value system.

That same sort of dynamic often shows up when a person starts to buy something—especially if it costs a great deal or if it represents a significant change in their lives.

Persons who have been renting for years, for example, may feel as if they are taking on the national debt when they sign a mortgage contract for a house. That buying decision may be a very sound one for them, but it will feel as if it is in violation of the values they have lived by for so long.

One of the real services you as a professional can render is to help them reconcile their choice with their value system. Thus, it is often helpful to explore very openly the fears they are feeling so they can become aware of their own value system and its limitations.

Buying Fear Reliever # 2:
Help Them Expand Their Own
Self-Belief

All of us have our own self-belief system—that imaginary world inside of which we feel safe, comfortable, and satisfied. Any time we start to do something that violates that world, we feel that we are on dangerous ground. As a result, we become afraid to try things that our emotions have not allowed us to experience owning before.

You can help your prospects overcome such fears by enabling them to reevaluate their own self-belief system. One way to do that is to focus for them how great the benefits of ownership will make them feel. Another way is to help them gradually experience what ownership will be like.

Buying Fear Reliever # 3:
Assure Them of the Wisdom of
Their Choices

Some people may be so self-confident that they don't feel hesitant to buy anything they want or need. However, those people are few and far between. For most people, buying is an unsettling experience.

A thousand questions may be rushing through a prospect's mind as he or she contemplates a decision to buy: Is this the right thing for me to do? What will so and so think about my decision? Can I pay for this thing? Is it really me? Do I really need it?

You can do prospects a big favor, and boost your chances for closing a sale, by reassuring them of the wisdom of their decision. Of course you can't tell them they are doing the right thing, any more than you can tell them that not buying is the wrong thing for them to do. You are not a judge, and you don't have to be. What you can do, however, is reassure them that they are making a wise decision—at least from a values perspective. Here are some ways you can do that.

First, you have to believe it yourself. That's one reason I'd have a hard time selling certain things to some people. For instance, I'd have a hard time selling expensive jewelry to someone whose children had on shabby shoes. If you know in your heart that a decision is not wise for a person, you are not much of a professional if you try to convince them otherwise. But if you know it's a wise decision, then reassure them with all your persuasive power.

Second, recap the benefits to show them how wise their decision is. You'll be amazed at how often a major benefit only dawns on a person the fifth or sixth time you repeat it. Don't assume they understand each benefit; make sure.

Third, reinforce all their positive feelings about buying. If they express a liking for some benefit, get them to talk more about it. If they are silent, ask them what they like most about what they've seen. Give them an opportunity to take psychological possession by asking them to tell you what they are looking forward to the most. The more they are talking positively about the benefits you've shown, the more they are selling themselves.

Fourth, answer any questions they may have. Honesty is always in order, but both honesty and complete openness are necessary during the Convince step. Stop everything you are doing and ask them if they have any questions they'd like to ask. Now is the time to find out if there are objections and what they are. In the next step, I'll share with you some insights on how to handle objections. But one thing you certainly never do is take them lightly. Deal with them as they come up, or they will act like ear muffs to block out everything you say.

One caution: If you ask for questions, then appear to hedge on an answer, that can destroy all the convincing you've done during this all-important step.

TO SUM IT ALL UP...

The Convince step is where you back up all the wonderful benefits you've promised the prospect; it's where you make them believe enough to act on your business proposal.

To do that, you must:

1. Prove your claims
2. Bring your own witnesses
3. Justify your price
4. Relieve the fear of buying

Now you're ready to tie it all up in an effective close. And that's what we'll talk about next.

ACTION STEPS

List at least one way you will use each of the four convincing actions we discovered in this chapter:

1. Prove your claims.
   ACTION PLAN: _____

2. Bring your own witnesses.
   ACTION PLAN: _____

3. Justify your price.
   ACTION PLAN: _____

4. Relieve the fear of buying.
   ACTION PLAN: _____

CHAPTER 9

Step Six: Tie It Up

How to Wrap Up
the Sale and
Take It Home

PURPOSE

There are four basic parts to the Tie-It-Up step:

1. Negotiate the conditions of the sale
2. Clear away objections
3. Ask for the order
4. Reinforce the sale

In this chapter, you will discover how to do each of those things.

> *"Closing is like when I kiss my wife.*
> *When it's right, I just do it;*
> *when it's not, I might as well not try!"*
> —*Veteran Salesman*

YOU TIE UP THE SALE, NOT THE CUSTOMER

I hate the expression *closing the sale* because it has become sales jargon for tying up the prospect, but that's not what it means at all.

Closing is not using clever gimmicks to trick people into something they really don't want to do. Neither is it the centerpiece of a sale, around which all other elements are built. Rather, tying up the sale is the natural outgrowth of doing the other five steps well. It's an orderly and simple step taken deliberately at the end of a series of steps. It can be fun—both for you and for the prospect.

"Closing is like when I kiss my wife," a wily old veteran of many sales once said in a seminar. "When it's right, I just do it; when it's not, I might as well not try!" With an attitude like that, you can get even the toughest customers to give you an order!

Remember that people want what you are selling, or they wouldn't buy it. They probably wanted it before you walked in. Perhaps they didn't know they wanted it until you showed them what they really wanted, or maybe you did such a good job that you made them want a particular model. At any rate, you cannot build a successful sales career by roping today's alert consumers and professional buyers into buying things they really don't want.

So, if they want it, and you want to sell it, then it's a simple process of tying up the loose ends of the transaction. As with each of the steps, there are certain tested and proven procedures you can follow. In this chapter, we will look at each of them.

I. NEGOTIATE THE CONDITIONS OF THE SALE

Successful negotiating is working out a mutually satisfactory agreement between two or more people for something they both want to do—it's handling the details in a way that enables everybody to win.

In a way, everything you have done up to this point has been a part of negotiating the sale. If you've followed the high impact selling system, you have already:

1. *Investigated* to discover who was interested in your business proposal
2. *Met* with prospects to enter into dialog on your proposal

3. *Probed* to find out what they wanted most and under what conditions they would buy it

4. *Applied* your most appropriate solution to their most compelling needs and desires

5. *Convinced* them that they can meet their needs and fulfill their wishes by buying whatever you are selling

That's the informal part of negotiating, and without it you cannot enter into formal negotiations. If you skip over any one of those steps, it will sabotage even your best efforts to *tie up the sale*.

If you have in fact completed the first five steps, you are now ready to start the formal negotiating process. Here are some winning strategies to help you become an effective negotiator.

Negotiation Strategy # 1:
Open the Negotiations on a Positive Note

A great time to open up the formal negotiations is right after your prospect has expressed approval or delight over some feature or benefit.

You simply ask, "Is there anything that would keep you from going ahead with this?" STOP!

I have found that to be the most useful question ever devised for opening up negotiations. It's a sincere and honest question, it cuts right through to the heart of the matter, and it is not in any way offensive. But the key to asking it properly is to stop after you've asked and wait for the prospect to respond. The question says it all. Be sure to listen very carefully to what the prospect says. If he or she says "No!" or "I don't see any reason not to go ahead," you can assume the close and begin writing up the sale. Very often, however, the prospect will show some hesitancy and offer some reason for not going ahead. If so, don't panic, just go to the next strategy.

Negotiation Strategy # 2:
Get All the Conditions on the Table

The prospect will almost never say, "I'll buy it under the following conditions." More often it will take the form, "I don't know! That's a lot of money!", "I wish you offered it in a different color." At this point, many salespeople react somewhat hysterically and start hammering away at all the reasons why it should not make a difference. That is a big mistake!

Such a response is a mistake because most stated conditions are only smokescreens to cover up deeper feelings of uncertainty. You simply cannot negotiate with a smokescreen—as soon as you satisfy one condition, the prospect will raise another.

Here's where you need to start probing again. It's the only way you can get all the conditions on the negotiating table so you can deal with them. Ask questions such as, "Is that the only reason you'd be hesitant to go ahead?" or "If I could show how to solve that problem, would you be ready to go ahead?" By pursuing this line of questioning you will eventually bring all the conditions out into the open.

Don't be afraid of this process. It's better to have negative feelings and thoughts come out at this stage than when you are trying to wrap up the sale. Once you feel you have all the conditions on the table, you can proceed to the next strategy.

Negotiation Strategy # 3: Make Sure You Understand the Conditions

Make sure you understand the conditions your prospect has listed. One good way to do it is to make a list of them and read them off to your prospect. Restate them in your own words and ask the prospect if you have really understood what he or she is feeling.

"Okay," you might say, "let me see if I understand what you've told me. . . . You feel uncertain that you can handle an expenditure of this size right now, and that you would prefer a different color. Is that right?"

It's important that you clearly understand what the prospect feels. It is equally important that the prospect understands what he or she feels. The only way you can reach that kind of understanding is through dialog. For example, you may surmise that a prospect is feeling, "I can't afford this," but what the person is actually feeling may be, "I can't justify spending that much money for such an item." There is a big difference between those two positions. Stay with the dialog process until you are confident that you and the prospect agree on what the stated conditions mean.

Negotiation Strategy # 4:
Offer to Try to Work Out Any Problems

At this point, you want to make it clear to your prospect that both of you are sitting on the same side of the negotiating table. In effect, you are saying: "I know you'd like to have the benefits I've shown you, and I know you have some concerns. I want to help you deal with those concerns so you can have the value I've created and the benefits you want." To do this, you simply agree with your client and offer to help him or her work out any problem.

Abraham Lincoln probably did this better than anyone in history, both a lawyer and a statesman. As a lawyer, he would sit and listen carefully to everything his opponent said. Then he'd slowly rise and address the jury. He'd start out by telling that panel how brilliant his opponent was, what a fine person he was, and how he had brought out some very valid points for the jurors to consider.

"However," he would gently add, "there are some other facts that need to be considered before you make a decision." Then he would set about to list skillfully all the reasons the jury should decide the case in favor of his client. More often than not, jurors said they felt old Abe was just helping them to reach an honest verdict.

The important thing is that you come out of the first strategy with (1) a clear understanding of the conditions under which the prospect will buy and (2) a strong trust bond between you and the prospect.

II. CLEAR AWAY OBJECTIONS

Objections are what I consider conditions that must be dealt with before a sale can be consummated. The way you handle objections will often determine whether or not you make the sale.

Almost always, a client will raise an objection from a feeling rather than a factual standpoint. Practically, this means that the salesperson needs to deal with objections forthrightly by addressing the feelings behind them. The salesperson who responds flippantly to a price objection by saying, "Sure it's a lot of money, but look what all you're getting!" is only asking for trouble.

I've discovered that the real reason most salespeople deal so poorly with objections is that they don't know how. All their training has focused on giving them canned responses to every objection that could possibly come up. They sound like a recorded message: "If prospect gives objection number four, you answer that with response number 67."

I want to show you how to handle objections like a real pro, so that you can do it with confidence from now on.

Objection Tactic # 1:
Simplify the Objection

At least half the work of solving any problem is to state that problem clearly and succinctly. Actually, when an objection is verbalized so that a prospect can really understand how he or she feels, it will most likely disappear.

Once when I was selling a land development program, a wealthy widow had objected to the idea of investing so much money. "What I hear you saying is that you don't feel you can justify investing that much money on a project like this, right?"

"That's right," she said thoughtfully. "Wait a minute! My husband is dead! Who do I have to justify it to?" she said with a big grin. She then snatched the pen out of my hand and said, "Where do I sign?"

It's not always that easy, but it always helps to know exactly what that prospect is feeling, and for them to know what they are feeling. That's what you achieve when you break an objection down to its simplest form and state it as a question.

Objection Tactic # 2:
Use the Feel, Felt, Found Formula

This is a technique that has been around for years, but it is still one strategy that I have found to be one of the most powerful ways to deal with objections. Here's how it works:

First, you say, "I understand how you feel about...." I've had clients actually look relieved and say, "You do?" It was as if they had expected me to tell them how silly it was for them to feel as they did.

You can say, "I understand how you feel," without the slightest fear of being dishonest. Even if you have never had precisely the same feelings, all of us know what it is like to feel some misgivings about a decision. If you had no empathy for the feelings of your prospects, you probably would not have persevered so far with the high impact method. Also, to understand does not mean to agree. You may think the feelings are totally unfounded, but you can totally understand the person's having them.

Next, you say, "Many of my clients felt the same way." It's like saying, "You're not an oddball," or "It's not unusual for someone to feel as you do." That takes a lot of pressure off clients and relieves them of feeling they have to defend their feelings. The net result is that they can look at their own feelings more objectively.

Since you understand, you have become their ally; and since you've known others who felt as they do, you can suggest ways they can deal with their feelings.

Finally, you say, "But they found. . . . " That opens the door to showing them how others have dealt with their feelings. You're not playing psychologist, just suggesting that others have found such feelings to be unfounded.

If you follow this three-step approach you have a powerful way to deal with objections that are based mainly on feelings.

Here's an example of how it can work:

"I understand how you feel about spending that much for a suit. . . . Many of my clients have felt it was a big investment. . . . But they found, since they enjoyed wearing it, they wore it more often and, since it lasted much longer than cheaper suits, their per wearing costs were actually lower." In a nutshell, what happens is that you

1. Accept the person's feelings
2. Assure the person that those feelings are valid and shared by others
3. Show the client that others have found those feelings to be unfounded because of one or more benefits of ownership

Objection Tactic # 3:
Make Sure They Understand All the Benefits

It is detrimental to assume a prospect understands all the benefits you've explained just because you've covered them several times. Make sure the person understands them.

I once learned this the hard way. I had received a call from an official of the Hanes Corporation who was considering booking me to

speak at an upcoming training sequence. I had used the same principles of high impact selling you are reading about and felt I had a good
chance of getting what I considered a great booking.

"I'm sure you'll do a good job for us, and your price is about what
others have quoted us," he said. "I'll get back with you after I've
talked with my boss."

Some time later, I hadn't heard from him, so I gave him a call.
"Oh, we went ahead and booked. . . . " Then he told me he'd sched-
uled a speaker whom I know and whose price is identical to mine.

"Do you mind if I ask what I did wrong?" I asked, quickly
noting, "It will help me know how to do a better job with other
people."

"Oh, you didn't do anything wrong," he assured me. "It's just
that his price included a pre-meeting survey to determine our needs."

I could have kicked myself! I always do a pre-meeting survey—
at no extra cost—and I know I had mentioned it to him, but I had
assumed he understood it. The other guy outsold me because he
made sure the client understood the benefit.

Objection Tactic # 4:
Test to See That the Objection Is Gone

Amateurs at selling brush aside objections with a canned response. Having swept them under the rug, they proceed as if there
were no conflicts in the client's mind. When they walk out without an
order, they wonder why the person didn't buy.

By contrast the real pros at selling always test to make sure
that each objection has been handled to the prospect's satisfaction.
They check to make sure it is gone and that it won't come back to
haunt them.

After you've used the "feel, felt, found formula," it's wise to ask
for the prospect's reaction: "Can you see how you might find the same
thing to be true for you?"

It's a simple test but it does two important things for you. First,
it lets you know if the objection is gone. If it's still there, you can use
the formula again and get more specific with it the next time around.
Second, it provides an opportunity for the prospect to verbalize his or
her own way of dealing with the objection. You'll be surprised how
often prospects will pick right up on it. "Sure, I remember a dress I

once bought that I thought would never wear out...and I always thought it made me look great!"

Now you're ready for the next big step.

III. ASK FOR THE ORDER

Everything you've done up to this point is wasted motion—unless you ask for the order. However, that's not as big a deal as many salespeople and trainers make it out to be. If you have followed carefully the first five steps—found out what your prospects want most and shown them how they can get it, and negotiated all the conditions necessary for the sale—asking for the order is a natural and logical step.

You can't make the buying decision for them, but you can facilitate the decision-making process for them. Let's look at some tested and proven techniques for making the buying decision easier for you and for your prospects.

Closing Technique # 1:
Use Trial Closes Throughout This Step

Sailors use what they call a "monkeyfist" to simplify what could be a tough task. The big ropes they use to tie a giant ocean liner up to a pier are often four to five inches thick, and they may weigh hundreds of pounds. Can you imagine how hard it would be to throw one of those little jewels from the ship to the pier? But the real problem would be for the guy on the other end to catch it.

So what sailors do is tie a little ball—called a "monkeyfist"—onto one end of a small rope and toss that over. The guy on the pier catches that with no problem, anchors it firmly, and starts pulling it in. Of course, the huge rope is tied to the other end and comes right along with it. Mission accomplished!

That's the best way I know to explain what a trial close is all about. You throw out test questions throughout the negotiation step. If the prospect grabs one and starts pulling on it, hook the close to it and wrap up the sale.

Actually, several of the questions we've discussed so far in this chapter are trial close questions. "Is there anything that would keep you from going ahead with this?" is a trial close. "Can you see how it might work the same way for you?" is another good one.

If you think about it, you can come up with some trial closes that feel perfectly natural for you. It's a good way to ease into asking for a buying decision.

Closing Technique # 2:
Ask Them to Buy Now

When you feel the time is right (and only you can *feel* it), just come right out and ask for the order. However, the way you ask for an order can either make it easier or more difficult for the prospect to make a buying decision.

Let me suggest a question that works fabulously for me and for thousands of other salespeople: "Is there anything that would keep you from buying now?"

There's nothing tricky about it. You don't need tricks if you've done a good job of selling. Asking for the order is merely a matter of tying up the loose ends of the sale. You look them straight in one eye, ask them to buy, and then shut up! You don't say another word until the prospect has responded.

Many salespeople are so afraid of rejection that they feel they must break any silence that lasts more than a few seconds. They may even jump in and say something illogical like: "Now I don't want to make you feel pressured," or "Maybe you want more time to think about this." All that does is delay the decision and possibly sabotage it permanently. Try to remember that some people just need a little space when they are making a decision.

Since some salespeople are reluctant to use such a direct close, however, let me give you the two other techniques that also work well.

Closing Technique # 3:
Assume the Sale

For many excellent salespeople, it works better to simply assume that the prospect has bought and start writing it up, all the while asking the prospect questions about details.

When you finish writing it up, you might ask, "Is there anything else we should include before we finalize the agreement?" If not, write the final price on the contract, mark a big "X" where the clients should sign, then hand it and your pen to them.

The chief advantage to this approach is that prospects never have to make one big decision to buy—just a series of little decisions—and many prospects feel much more comfortable with that. The chief disadvantage is that some people feel pressured if they are not quite ready to make a decision. If that happens, lay the contract aside and start probing to find out why they are hesitant.

Closing Technique # 4:
Use the Either/Or Close

Another way to make it easy for prospects to decide to buy is to give them a choice other than "yes" or "no". You can do this with the alternative close, also known as the either/or close.

It works like this: You ask for a question that lets them choose between having it one way or another. "Do you like it best in red, or would you rather have the blue?" "Can I schedule delivery on Wednesday, or do you prefer that I schedule it for next Monday?" "Do you prefer to pay cash, or would you rather use our convenient easy payment plan?"

One good way to lead into it is to summarize the benefits and state the price just before you ask the question. Another good approach is to ask the question immediately after the prospect has made a positive statement about some feature or benefit he or she particularly likes.

The greatest advantage of the assumptive close is that it shields people from ever having to make a buying decision as such—they simply choose which model they want or the conditions under which to buy. It's probably the closing technique in which most prospects will feel the least pressure.

Closing Technique # 5:
Deal with Fear of Making a Decision

Often you will find that a prospect is sold on the product, feels comfortable with all the conditions of the purchase, but is simply hesitant to make a buying decision.

In such cases, it is crucial that you not make the person feel rushed. I had one prospect who stopped me and said: "Look! If you can give me a few minutes to think about this, I might say 'yes'. If you have to know right now, the answer is NO!"

"Take as much time as you like!" I said, with a great big smile. I quickly laid the contract aside, we talked for 20 minutes about her family, then she signed the order without a moment's hesitation.

If you sense there is more than needing a little time or space to make a decision, it's a good idea to probe into exactly why the person is hesitant. If you discover there is some key issue that must be settled, try to settle it just as you would handle any objection and go on with the close.

Usually it helps to focus that key issue as precisely as possible. You can do that by asking, "If it were not for the balloon note at the end of the lease agreement, would you be ready to go ahead with this?"

If the prospect says "yes," then you know exactly what you are dealing with and can try to negotiate a new set of conditions he/or she could accept. If not, you need to keep probing until you pin down that one key factor and deal with it.

IV. REINFORCE THE SALE

Once a prospect makes a decision to buy, many salespeople start packing up and getting out as fast as they can. Them seem to feel they should split before the prospect changes his or her mind.

Believe me, if those customers want to back out, they'll find a way to back out—no matter what they've signed. What's more, your haste to get out of there can damage the trust bond you've worked so hard to create. It's better to take a few minutes to tie up some loose ends before you leave.

Reinforcement # 1:
Compliment Them on Their Choice

Saying "I think you've made a very wise choice" is a simple, yet very effective way to reinforce the sale.

What makes it so helpful is that it not only congratulates purchasers, but opens the door for them to express their own positive feelings about their purchase. The more they talk about it, the more comfortable they will become with their decision.

This self-acknowledgment can help to head off several problems. For example, if a client's decision is later questioned by someone the person respects, the client will have become resolute enough in the decision that he or she is not likely to be talked out of it.

Reinforcement # 2:
Invite Them to Buy More

Very often the best prospect for a sale is the very client to whom you've just sold your product or service.

A friend and colleague of mine tells the story of the day he bought his first Mercedes automobile some years ago. He'd given the man a check for about $40,000 for a sedan, and was standing in his lobby chatting with the young salesman and his sales manager.

The young fellow was evidently still in training, but it was the sales manager's anxiety that was in evidence as he kept trying to hurry my friend out the door.

"You've made a wise investment and I think you are in for a real treat when you discover what's so special about owning a Mercedes," the young salesman said.

"Thanks, I'm sure I'll enjoy it!" my colleague replied.

"In fact, there's only one way you can make a better decision than the one you've just made," the salesman mused. At this, the sales manager rolled his eyes toward the ceiling as if to say, "What am I going to do with this kid!"

"How's that?" my friend asked.

"Go ahead and let me deliver that 450SL sports model we talked about for your wife, too!" he said with a grin.

"I'll tell you what!" he said after thinking for a minute. "You find me a metallic gray with a blue top and you've just sold yourself another car!"

Chuckling about it later, my friend said, "I suspect that young salesman almost wet his pants right there in my lobby."

"When was the last time you sold two cars, worth $80,000, in about 15 minutes?" he asked the sales manager as he handed him a second check.

"Never!" came the instant reply. It might very well have been because he'd never dared to ask anyone to buy a second car.

The point is that you never know until you ask. A person who is sold on a product might add on to the sale, might upgrade their choice, or might even duplicate it.

Reinforcement # 3:
Assure Them of Satisfaction

It's also a good idea to reassure your clients that they are not alone in dealing with a bunch of strangers from some company they can hardly make contact with. "I'll check back with you next week to make sure you got everything okay" can reassure them that they're not dealing with an impersonal organization. You might want to add, "If you have any problems with delivery, feel free to call me."

However, if you promise to check back with them, make sure you do. If there is a problem, and you don't check back, you'll only compound the anger they feel.

Reinforcement # 4:
Ask for Their Help

Interestingly, one of the best ways to reinforce the sale is immediately to ask the prospect for help. It's also a good way to pick up some great leads and introductions.

You can simply say, "I know you are going to enjoy wearing this new outfit. And you probably have some friends who have tastes that are similar to yours. Do you mind if I call on some of them and mention your name as a satisfied customer?" Then pick up your leather binder and pen and get ready to write.

If they agree, they will probably start mentioning names. Ask them questions about the people they recommend and make notes you will find useful when you start calling on them.

You can watch their reactions and consider carefully your next step. Some salespeople I know will say, "You know, sometimes there are several people in town with the same name, and I often have trouble finding the right person. Do you mind taking a few minutes to help me find these people in the phone book, so I'll avoid the embarrassment of calling the wrong person?"

If you feel the person is really getting into helping you, you might even ask them to call one or two of their friends and introduce you to them. If you think it's appropriate, you can ask them to give you a letter of endorsement.

You'd be surprised how this can cement your relationship with your new customer—and give you some dynamite leads!

TO SUM IT ALL UP...

Remember, there are four basic parts to the Tie-It-Up step:

1. Negotiate the conditions of the sale
2. Clear away objections
3. Ask for the order
4. Reinforce the sale

You can't take that step until you've carefully done each of the preceding five steps. It's as if you've earned the right to close the sale only when you have

1. *Investigated* to discover who was interested in your business proposal
2. *Met* with prospects to enter into dialog on your proposal
3. *Probed* to find out what they wanted most and under what conditions they would buy it
4. *Applied* your most appropriate solution to their most compelling needs and desires
5. *Convinced* them that they can meet their needs and fulfill their wishes by buying whatever you are selling

Add the *Tie-It-Up* step, and you've got IMPACT—the high impact selling system—the most powerful selling system ever devised.

Next, we'll take a look at some basic guidelines for making the system work for you.

ACTION STEPS

Set a goal for improving your closing techniques by using each of the following procedures:

1. Negotiate the conditions of the sale.
   GOAL _____

2. Clear away objections.
   GOAL _____

3. Ask for the order.
   GOAL _____

4. Reinforce the sale.
   GOAL _____

CHAPTER 10

How to Put High Impact Selling to Work for You

PURPOSE

The high impact selling system, like any procedure, works only when you make it work. In this chapter, we'll examine:

1. An overview of the high impact selling system
2. Why it's so powerful
3. Some guidelines to help you make it work for you

> *It's good to work hard,*
> *better to work smart,*
> *but best to work hard*
> *and smart.*

WORKING SMART IN A CRAZY WORLD

You work hard, I'm sure. If you weren't a go-getter, you probably wouldn't have read this far. But perhaps you are like many of the salespeople I've met in my seminars who weren't getting all they deserved for all the hard work they were doing. Their problem had nothing to do with attitude, or with motivation, or even with sincerity. They were just incompetent at selling.

Now, don't let that word *incompetent* scare you off; it simply means "without adequate skill or knowledge." I'd be an incompetent brain surgeon, airline pilot, or truck driver because I'm "without adequate skill or knowledge" for those professions.

Unfortunately, many of those hardworking salespeople had been beaten over the head so often by sales managers and trainers using outmoded selling systems designed for the 1950s that they were discouraged and absolutely without self-confidence. Others had worked like crazy, but had no system to work with. The sad fact is that incompetence mobilized is nothing more than mobilized incompetence.

A Game Plan for Working Hard and Smart

That's precisely why I developed the high impact selling system—to give honest, hardworking salespeople a game plan with which they could succeed.

Interestingly, as I've started teaching it in seminars and sales meetings all over the country, I've discovered it can be just as helpful to salespeople who've been quite successful but open to discovering a better way of doing things. They're the easiest to sell on the high impact selling system because they recognize right off how powerful it really is. As they start implementing it in their own careers, they find they are working shorter hours but making more sales.

To make sure you understand what the system is, how powerful it is, and how to make it work for you, let me offer some pointers I think you'll find useful.

I. AN OVERVIEW OF THE HIGH IMPACT SELLING SYSTEM

The high impact selling system gives you an alphabet of professional techniques designed for today's new selling environment:

Investigate to discover who is interested in your business proposal.

Meet with prospects to enter into dialog on your proposal.

Probe to find out what they want most and under what conditions they will buy it.

Apply your most appropriate solution to their most compelling needs and desires.

Convince them that they can fulfill their needs and wishes by buying whatever you are selling.

Tie It Up and take it home.

Put them all together and you've got IMPACT; the most powerful selling system ever devised.

II. WHY IT'S SO POWERFUL

Remember, I said you should never make a claim you could not back up, so let me back up my claim that the high impact selling system is the most powerful selling system ever devised.

For some time now, I've been training salespeople for the Chevrolet Division of General Motors, Inc., using the same basic system I've explained to you. Salespeople for many of my client dealers are now closing as high as 40 percent of the prospects they pitch, while the national closing average is only 17 percent.

What makes it so powerful? There's no mystery to it, no magic, not even any trickery. It's a commonsense approach that is in touch with today's alert shopper.

Let's look at some reasons it works so well:

1. *It's simple to learn and easy to remember.*

My philosophy of education is pretty down to earth: *You can't learn what you don't understand, and you can't remember what you don't know.*

Any person of average intelligence can understand everything I've explained in each of the steps. You've probably already memorized the acronym IMPACT. If not, all you have to do is repeat it aloud a dozen times and you've got it forever. Each of the step names is self-explanatory and describes precisely what you do.

2. *It's built on sound selling principles that have been tested and proven effective.*

A lot of selling systems can boast of being simple and easy to remember. Catchy but empty slogans often stick in your mind with little effort to learn them and less benefit from the ideas behind them. High impact selling, however, is worth learning because it is built on sound selling principles that have been proven effective.

Even if you should forget the specific words I've used, you will be able to express their meaning in your own words. Perhaps even more importantly, you will be able to use the concepts to become increasingly effective.

3. *It's comprehensive.*

One beautiful thing about sound principles is that the more you study them, the deeper you discover they are. They're like pieces of great classical music — every time you hear them, you learn something new.

A cursory reading of each chapter outlining one of the steps will give you all the insight you need to get started. Yet you can read through a chapter a dozen times and learn something new with each reading.

4. *It's customer centered.*

Unlike most sales training, which is based on products, companies, or gimmicks — and unlike most sales motivation systems which are built around the self — the high impact selling system is customer centered. It recognizes the customer as the single most important ingredient in selling and bases everything on appealing to and serving that customer. It is designed to give you high impact where it counts — with your prospects! That's why I've chosen to call it the high impact selling system.

5. *It's values focused.*

People's value systems differ greatly not only from individual to individual but from generation to generation. Any effort to deliver values that are appropriate to those ever-changing value systems must be both perceptive and creative. The high impact selling system gives you a central focus that enables you to appeal to your most discriminating customers.

6. *It's adaptable.*

If a selling system is to meet the wide variety of needs of many different selling styles, situations, and markets, it must be highly flexible. You will find that the high impact selling system adapts easily to fit any personality, any product or service, any clientele, and that it fits equally well in stores, door-to-door selling, industrial sales, and any other selling situation.

What's more it is timeless in the sense that it will be just as useful in the 90s and beyond as it is today.

7. *It's honest and direct.*

Perhaps most important of all, the high impact selling system is an honest and direct approach that is sure to appeal to both sophisticated shoppers and nonmanipulative salespeople. It removes the need for cheap gimmickry, tricky openings and closings, and exaggerated claims. To use Ron Willingham's great term, it is "integrity selling" of the highest order. Now even the most sincere and gentle person can become a powerful salesperson.

But it is also direct enough that even the most aggressive salespeople can use its basic principles and techniques.

Now, let's look at some tips on making the system work for you.

III. HOW TO MAKE THE SYSTEM WORK WELL FOR YOU

Most selling systems concern themselves with getting you to memorize myriads of slogans, tricks, and snappy answers. You know how it goes: "If the prospect says this, you say that!"

They remind me of the story about the salesman who was stranded on a deserted road and walked five miles to the first house. Seeing no one around and noticing that the door was open, he knocked on the door molding.

"Come on in, big boy! Come on in, big boy!" a voice kept repeating from deep inside the house.

Following the voice, he cautiously made his way down a long hall to what appeared to be a bedroom.

"Come on in, big boy!" came the voice from inside the room. Slowly he pushed the door open.

Suddenly he found himself pinned to the wall by a huge Doberman pinscher. In a cage in the opposite corner of the room sat a parrot who kept saying "Come on in, big boy!"

"Don't you know how to say anything but 'Come on in, big boy!'?" the salesman asked nervously.

"Attack! Attack!" said the parrot.

That's about the way many salespeople have learned to sell. You say, "Boy, are you lucky today!" until the prospect asks if you don't know anything else to say. Then you start shouting, "Gimme' an order! Gimme' an order!"

Well, you can relax! My goal is not to make a parrot out of you: It is to show you how to become a highly competent salesperson by giving you the skills and knowledge to sell almost anybody almost anything.

Tip # 1: Use the System to Learn the System

One thing I find so exciting about the high impact selling system is that it can not only be used for selling—it provides a great strategy for a wide range of uses.

For example, you can use the basic steps of the system to learn how to use the system. Let me show you how it works:

Investigate your own selling situation to determine what you need to do to become more effective at selling your products to your market.

Meet the system by learning the six basic steps.

Probe into the system to study all the tools it gives you.

Apply each of those tools to your own selling needs.

Convince yourself that the system really works with whatever you are selling.

Tie It Up and take it home by putting into practice what you have learned.

When you get it all together, you've got high personal and professional IMPACT.

Isn't that simple? Try using the whole system to learn how to boost your batting average, or use it to improve specific steps of the selling process, such as prospecting or closing. It really works!

Tip # 2: Follow Three Simple Guidelines

If you'll follow these three simple guidelines, you'll be amazed at how well high impact selling can work for you.

1. Don't be impatient—always follow the formula in sequence.
2. Complete each step fully before proceeding to the next step.
3. Identify where you are at all times and be sure that you and your prospect are always at the same point in the process.

It's sometimes helpful to retreat a step or two. For example, if you are in the Tie-It-Up step and discover through a trial close that your prospect has a conflicting desire you had not discovered, go back to the Probe step and explore that desire with him or her.

On the other hand, it is almost never productive to jump ahead one or more steps. The obvious exception would be if a prospect said, "I'm ready to buy," while you were still in the second step. In that case, you don't need anybody's system—you need an order blank!

Tip # 3: Use the System Consistently

The more you use the high impact selling system, the better you'll become at it. At first, it might feel a little stilted to you, but by the second or third time you use it, you will feel right at home with it.

One big advantage of such an open-ended and flexible system is that you can always grow with it. If you are a mediocre salesperson now, you can become good by using the high impact selling system. By repeated practice, you can become great—eventually even superb!

My only real concern is getting you to start using it now. Once you've tried it for a few days, you'll find it boosts your selling power so much that you wouldn't even consider using anything else.

TO SUM IT ALL UP...

Just to make sure you understand the high impact selling system, let me give it to you one more time:

Investigate to discover who is interested in your business proposal.

Meet with prospects to enter into dialog on your proposal.

Probe to find out what they want most and under what conditions they will buy it.

Apply your most appropriate solution to their most compelling needs and desires.

Convince them that they can fulfill their needs and wishes by buying whatever you are selling.

Tie It Up and take it home.

Put them all together and you've got IMPACT—the most powerful selling system ever devised.

Go ahead! Try it! You'll like it!

ACTION STEPS

1. Memorize the six steps of the high impact selling system if you have not already done so.

2. Set a target date for having it fully operational in your own selling.
   TARGET DATE: _____

How to Master Personal Management Skills

PURPOSE

Now that you have discovered how to boost your customer impact and have learned how to master selling skills, I'm ready to give you the third power strategy for success in selling, namely, how to master personal management skills.

In this section you'll learn

1. How to make more sales in less time
2. How to keep yourself going when the going gets tough
3. How to enjoy all the success you achieve

HOW TO TURN WHAT YOU KNOW INTO WHAT
YOU CAN SPEND

"If you're so darned smart, why ain't you rich?" reads the sign on a beat-up old truck I see around my hometown occasionally.

It's a good question. Whether you are poor and want to be rich, or rich and want to be richer, you'll find some very useful information in this section of the book.

But maybe your concern is not so much money, but that you seem to always be working hard, yet never seem to get anywhere. Perhaps you are like I was once, I'd work 14 to 16 hours every day, and on most weekends, yet I was always behind in everything I was doing. The frustrating part of it was that I wasn't doing anything very well and I couldn't seem to break the pattern.

Then I discovered something that radically changed all that. I discovered that the only way I could control my life was to manage the way I spent every minute of every day. It wasn't that I had not known what to do or how to do it, my problem was that I never seemed to find enough time to get around to doing what I knew I should.

After this discovery I decided to do an in-depth study of time management principles and put them to work in my own life. The difference it made was dramatic, to say the least. I'm now working fewer hours, getting more done, and enjoying it a whole lot more.

If you want to know how to make more sales, in less time, and with less effort, turn the page and let's get going.

CHAPTER 11

How to Make More Sales in Less Time

PURPOSE

You can use the basic principles of the high impact selling system to deal effectively with every area of your life. In this chapter, I want to show you how to use it to gain complete control over your time rather than allowing time to hold you hostage. You'll discover how to:

1. Investigate to determine your need for better time management
2. Meet your own time habits head on
3. Probe time-wasting habits
4. Apply time management techniques to your selling career
5. Convince yourself that you can gain control of your time
6. Tie it up by putting it into practice in your daily life

> *"There is a tide in the affairs of men,*
> *Which, taken at the flood, leads on to fortune;*
> *Omitted, all the voyage of their life*
> *Is bound in shallows and miseries.*
> *On such a full sea are we now afloat,*
> *And we must take the current where it serves,*
> *Or lose our ventures."*
> *—William Shakespeare*

HOW TO PROTECT YOUR PRIME TIME

They call it *prime time*. The major television networks diligently guard the hours from eight to eleven each night. They know that's when they will have their largest audiences and thus when they can make the most money by selling commercials.

Salespeople have certain times each day that offer greater opportunities than any other time during that day. They are the precious minutes you spend before your prospect, actually selling. It's your prime selling time!

Yet, if you are like most salespeople I know, there are at least 1001 things that are constantly trying to snatch away your prime time. All too often, life's little urgencies win the battle and take away those invaluable moments. According to a recent study by Columbia University, for example, the typical salesperson spends less than 90 minutes every day before prospects actually promoting his or her products.

The conclusion we draw from this can be expressed by this principle:

> Time Management Principle # 1:
> The more you do of what you're doing, the more you'll get of what you've got!

What if you could double, or even triple, your prime time? What if you could do more of the things that can get you what you want out of life?

You can do exactly that if you will use the principles of the high impact selling system to gain control of your time. Let's explore how it works.

I. INVESTIGATE YOUR NEED FOR BETTER TIME MANAGEMENT

I could give you countless slogans and cliches about how important it is to utilize every minute of every day to its maximum advantage, but you know how important it is or you wouldn't be reading this chapter.

Rather, I'll give you some practical ideas that have worked well for me and thousands of other people. Hopefully, you'll find some insights you can use to investigate your own needs.

Understanding Time Management

Technically, we can't manage time at all because we have no control over it. This is expressed very poignantly by Henry Austin Dobson in "Paradox of Time":

> "Time goes, you say? Ah no!
> Alas, Time stays, we go."

All we can really do is to manage our use of time. When we speak of time management, then, we are actually talking about self-management.

Where Does Your Time Go?

Most of us manage our money down to the last penny. We draw up budgets and discipline ourselves to live by them. If we don't, we'll soon find ourselves broke and head over heels in debt. Unfortunately, far too many salespeople fail to apply the same principles of guarding and utilizing their prime selling time—even though it's much more valuable than money.

The most pressing question about activities is not "What are you doing?" but "Why are you doing it?" You can work hard all day every day and still not get much done. The question is not, "How hard do you work?" but "What do you work at doing?" "Busy work" is not productive because it doesn't go anywhere—no matter how much time and energy it eats up.

To be successful in selling you have to focus on your goals, not on your activities. If you constantly feel yourself rushing like mad and still coming up short on time, chances are pretty good you need to do something about your personal time management habits and practices.

II. MEETING YOUR TIME HABITS HEAD ON

The first step in managing your life is knowing precisely where it goes. Sure, most of us can have a general idea of where our time goes. We know we work so many hours each day, we sleep so many hours, we spend some time eating, and so forth.

But how do we spend our time working? Or playing? Or doing anything else? The fact is that most of us simply don't know.

Let me suggest a very effective tactic for analyzing your time habits: Keep a detailed time log for a definite period and carefully analyze what you do with your time.

Before you say, "I don't have time to mess with that," and brush the idea aside, let me tell you some of the fantastic benefits of keeping a time log:

1. You'll discover some holes you can plug and save a bundle of your prime selling time.

2. You'll probably find there are certain times of the day, and certain days of the week, you tend to waste more time than others. So you can improve your scheduling.

3. When you discover how much time you spend on certain activities, you might feel it is all out of proportion to their significance. For example, you might find you spend 80 percent of your time calling on people who account for only 20 percent of your sales. You can then begin looking for ways to cut the time you spend with marginal accounts.

4. You might also discover some very important customers who are being slighted, and you can plan to give them the time they deserve.

5. You'll only have to do it periodically for it to be very helpful to you.

Keeping a time log is really quite simple. All you do is write down what you do during each quarter hour or so of whatever time you're logging. Be careful not to change your regular routines so you'll get an accurate picture.

After you've kept a detailed log for two weeks or so, look it over very carefully. Analyze specifically which activities get the most amounts of time and rate them as to priorities. Search for time-wasting actions and loopholes. Study the amount of time you spend with certain people and decide if it's justified.

You can use the time log to study everything about the way you spend your time. Believe me, if you'll take it seriously, two weeks of keeping a time log will completely change the way you relate to using your time. it will enable you to meet your own time habits head on.

III. PROBE TO DISCOVER YOUR TIME-WASTING HABITS

Time-wasting habits can rob you of your most vital possession—your very own life—and give little or nothing in return. If you really want to gain control of your time, you simply must discover your personal time-wasting habits.

Here's an excellent tactic for discovering the activities that most frequently waste your time. Keep a running list of all time-wasting activities you notice during the next week. Each time you find yourself engaging in a time-waster, write down the amount of time you waste. Then add up the total times of each of your biggest time wasters. You might find it very revealing.

Watch for such notorious time thieves as:

1. Procrastinating—putting things off until they end up re-quiring more time or until they gang up on you and take control of your schedule
2. Doing unnecessary routine tasks—just because you've al-ways done them
3. Unnecessary distractions or interruptions
4. Inefficient use of the telephone
5. Unnecessary meetings, or meetings that last too long
6. Lack of self-discipline in matters of time
7. Excessive socializing, and stretching your lunch and refresh-ment breaks

   8. Lack of knowledge about your job

   9. Failure to set and live by priorities

 10. Making careless mistakes that necessitate redoing work

 11. Daydreaming at the wrong times

 12. Unnecessary shuffling of mail and paperwork

That's the "dirty dozen" list of the most frequent ways people waste time. You might be able to add several to the list, and maybe you don't waste time in all the most common ways listed above. The important thing is that you identify the ways you waste time and then eliminate them one by one until they are all gone.

IV. APPLY TIME MANAGEMENT TECHNIQUES TO YOUR SELLING CAREER

The master key to all effective time management is *planning*. That word scares many people, but it need not scare you. Planning simply means using a systematic strategy of applied consistency. In other words, plan your life through setting priorities and then live your plan. Here are some planning tips that have helped thousands of salespeople get more done in less time.

   1. *Make planning a way of life*

   Planning your time is deciding in advance what you're going to do and how you're going to do it, allocating the time needed to get it done, and following the plan you have laid. What's important is that you do it and that you apply it to every area of your life.

   2. *Put yourself on a schedule*

   Most salespeople, given the choice, would probably rather live without a schedule. Unfortunately, there is no such thing as un-scheduled living. You either decide your own schedule or let other people or circumstances decide it for you.

   Actually, a schedule is nothing to be feared: It's simply a road-map to guide you through the day. Of course, the more complete it is, the more it can help you save time. For example, instead of merely setting aside certain hours for work, why not allocate definite time periods to accomplish specific tasks?

3. *Get your whole life organized*

Many of the least successful salespeople in the world are not lazy—they're just disorganized. In fact, most salespeople work much harder than they need to because they are so disorganized. They work frantically all day, conscientiously try to get everything done, and leave work tense because of important clients not seen and reports unfinished.

Getting organized can help you work more easily, get more done, and make you more valuable to any sales organization. It keeps you from reinventing the wheel every time you need a ride, from wasting energy and time on lost motion, and from feeling frustrated because you can't find things.

Here are some ideas that can help you get organized and stay that way:

Don't just shuffle papers—process them: Picking up the same piece of paper again and again is a waste of time. If it's important enough to act upon, act. If it's not important enough for a decision, either file it or throw it away.

Keep your life uncluttered: I love the philosophy of Andy Rooney, the jovial grouch of "Sixty Minutes." He says he has a rule that for everything new that comes in the front door, something of equal size has to go out the back door. It's not a bad idea.

Excessive clutter complicates every task, wastes valuable time, and leads to mistakes. You'll be amazed at how much your productivity will improve, and how much more you'll enjoy your whole life, if you'll simply designate a place for everything and keep everything in its designated place.

Practice decisiveness: One thing that keeps people from being organized is that they hate to make decisions. Don't flounder around all day sorting through more and more facts; gather a reasonable amount of information, study it, then make a decision.

Sure, you'll make mistakes. The only way to keep from making mistakes is to do nothing, and that's the biggest mistake of all. Besides, studies show that decisive people actually make fewer mistakes than people who struggle endlessly over every choice they must make.

V. CONVINCE YOURSELF THAT YOU CAN GAIN CONTROL OF YOUR TIME

You, and only you, can gain complete control of your time. I've always thought of myself as a hard worker. In fact, I seemed always to be rushing around frantically trying to get everything done. I lived under constant stress and had developed numerous stress-related problems, including colitis.

Then in 1979 I attended a time-management seminar and discovered why I was having to work so hard so long every day. My problem was that, while I was working very hard, I was not working very smart.

Let me share with you some of the most valuable insights I gained from that seminar—and from experience since that time.

1. *Concentrate on results, not on activities*

As a coach, I always chose my starting line-up on the basis of one overriding principle: I wanted the 22 players who would consistently give me their peak performance when it counted most—during the games. Now I was about to apply that same principle to my own life and work. I needed to be at my best at those times that called for my best performance—my prime time.

That's when I discovered the simple, but profound, Pareto Principle, which says that 80 percent of one's results derive from 20 percent of one's activities. What if, I began to reason, I could consciously devote 80 percent of my time to the accomplishment of those activities that accounted for 80 percent of my results? The idea was astounding! That would mean I could achieve peak effectiveness 80 percent of the time. So that's exactly what I started trying to achieve. It has made me much more productive and given me much more spare time.

Think for a moment what that could mean in your own selling career. It would mean that you could spend 80 percent of your time actually before prospects closing sales. What's more, it would mean that you would spend 80 percent of your prime time with the 20 percent of your clients who produce 80 percent of your sales volume.

What makes it all possible is getting and keeping your priorities straight. You have to think RESULTS! That means you have to learn how to weed out all the nonproductive activities which eat up so much valuable time, and focus all your efforts on doing the most productive task, at the most productive time, and in the most productive way.

Try it! It really works!

2. *Learn to use the myriads of time-saving devices available today*

You might be amazed at how much of your prime time might be saved by better use of dictating and answering machines, personal computers and word processors, paging services, and so on.

3. *Develop time awareness*

Most of us let many precious moments slip away each hour because we simply don't pay attention to where they go.

To correct this, each time you find yourself wasting time, imagine an alarm going off inside and charge yourself an imaginary fine of a dollar. Total it up at the end of the day to see how much it has cost you. To see how much your time is worth, consult the chart below and locate the income you want to earn.

It takes a little effort to become time conscious, but it pays rich dividends.

Time Value Chart

Annual Income	Each Hour Is Worth	Each Minute Is Worth	An Hour a Day for a Year Is Worth
$ 20,000	10.32	.1728	$ 2,518
$ 25,000	12.81	.2134	$ 3,125
$ 30,000	15.37	.2561	$ 3,750
$ 35,000	17.93	.2988	$ 4,375
$ 40,000	20.64	.3596	$ 5,036
$ 50,000	25.62	.4268	$ 6,250
$ 75,000	38.42	.6404	$ 9,375
$100,000	51.22	.8538	$12,499

Note: The table is based on 244 working days of 8 hours each. By saving one hour each working day during a normal career, you can add the equivalent of six years of productivity. That's better than retiring early, with full benefits.

4. *Learn to use little tidbits of time productively*

What do you do when you have to wait for someone, even when you have an appointment? Or when you get stuck in traffic jams, or take long rides on airliners or other conveyances?

It's easy to sit and stew away precious minutes (even hours) when that happens. That's letting circumstances and people run your life. You can rescue that lost time by always keeping handy some worthwhile tasks to do. For example, it's a good time to catch up on your chosen reading (not on the outdated and irrelevant magazines usually available in waiting rooms). Or you can use that time to do some of your routine paperwork.

If you are creative about it, you can process some of your best ideas or write down new ones. Noel Coward, while stranded in a traffic jam, took out a pen and paper and wrote "I'll See You Again," one of his greatest songs.

Don't just sit there and stew. Use your imagination to come up with productive uses for any time you spend waiting for someone or something beyond your control. It will not only save you time, it will help you keep stress under control.

5. *Keep your priorities straight with "to do" lists*

A "to do" list is one of the simplest and most effective devices for managing your time. Simply take a few minutes at the end of each day to write down the five to ten *most important* things you need to get done the next day; then arrange them numerically according to priority. The next morning, start with your number one priority and move on through the list until you've done them all. As simple as it is, it can do wonders to save you time and help you avoid frustration.

"This is the most practical lesson I've ever learned," said Charles Schwab, the founder of Bethlehem Steel, to a group of budding young executives. "I had put off making a phone call for nine months," he explained, "so I decided to list it as my number one task on the next day's agenda. That call netted us $2 million because of a new order for steel beams."[1] From that moment on, Mr. Schwab became an avid fan of "to do" lists—and I think you'll agree he was a pretty good salesman.

Living by "to do" lists is the best way to ensure that you concentrate on what's *really important*, not on things that only *seem urgent* at the moment.

6. *Enjoy your free time*

[1] Charles Schwab, in Nido R. Qubein, *Get the Best from Yourself* (Englewood Cliffs, N.J.: Prentice-Hall, 1983), p. 89.

You'll be a better salesperson if you face up to the fact that you owe it to yourself, to your loved ones, and even to your bosses to get plenty of rest and recreation. It's the only way you can be your best.

Nowhere is self-discipline more important than in the matter of taking time to recharge your batteries. Your body, mind, and psyche are structured so that they must have time to renew themselves; otherwise, you will always be operating below your capacity.

Dale Carnegie, one of the all-time great success motivators, often used a story to illustrate this point.[2] Two woodcutters were hired to clear a large tract of land. One fellow worked at breakneck speed all day while the other stopped every hour or so to take a break. At the end of the first day, the frantic worker noticed that the other fellow's pile of wood was much larger than his.

"I don't understand!" he complained. "My axe has struck every time yours has today. Besides, I've worked straight through, while you sat down for about five minutes out of every hour.... Yet you've cut more wood than I have!"

"Did you notice," said the wise old wood cutter, "that while I was sitting, I was sharpening my axe?"

That's what relaxing is all about—it's sharpening your axe so you can work more effectively.

VI. TIE IT UP BY PUTTING IT IN PRACTICE IN YOUR DAILY LIFE

There has never been a system devised that will work—unless someone makes it work.

The story is told of a group of salespeople who were stranded in a motel during a terrible snowstorm. As salespeople often do, they all gathered in the bar to talk about their troubles.

"What's the weather doing out there?" they'd ask each newcomer.

Finally, one old veteran of years of traveling walked in and someone asked, "Do you think we'll be able to get out of here tomorrow?"

"That all depends?" he drawled.

"On what?" they asked.

[2] Ibid., p. 153.

"It depends on whether you're on salary or straight commission!" he said drily.

Make no mistake about it: You work for yourself, no matter who signs your checks. Whether you are on salary or commission, your income will ultimately be determined by one thing—how seriously you take the tips in this chapter.

If you'll take them seriously enough to put them in practice in your daily life, I'll promise you that you will become as successful at selling as you wish to become.

ACTION STEPS

1. Make a list of the most common ways you waste time each week, a method for overcoming each, and an estimate of the time you could save by eliminating the wasteful practice. At the end, add up the time you could save during a typical week. Then figure (based on your weekly income level) how much money you could save by plugging the gaps.

2. *IF YOU'RE REALLY SERIOUS....* Start immediately keeping a time log, and analyze your time habits for the next two weeks. Then develop strategies to get better control of your time usage. It'll save you loads of time in the weeks and years to come.

Time Waster	Time Saver	Time Saved
_____	_____	_____
_____	_____	_____
_____	_____	_____
_____	_____	_____
_____	_____	_____
_____	_____	_____
_____	_____	_____
_____	_____	_____
_____	_____	_____
_____	_____	_____
_____	_____	_____
_____	_____	_____

Total time to be saved weekly: _____

Net value of time saved: _____

CHAPTER 12

How to Cash in on the Power of Enthusiasm

PURPOSE

Your personal and professional impact will depend greatly on the enthusiasm with which you approach the high impact selling system—and your whole career. In this final chapter, I want to share some thoughts with you on:

1. What enthusiasm is
2. How to get it and keep it

> *"Nothing great was
> ever accomplished
> without enthusiasm."*
> —*Ralph Waldo Emerson*

I. WHAT IS ENTHUSIASM?

For many salespeople, the word *enthusiasm* has become a real loser because it has too often been associated with the hoopla some have used to whip them into a frenzy. Yet it's a good solid word with a rich heritage. It was coined to describe what appeared to be superhuman performances by Olympic athletes in ancient Greece, and came from a compound Greek word—"en + theos"—and means "enabled by the gods."

Enthusiasm is a deep inner drive to excel at doing a task or reaching a goal. The real enthusiasts concentrate all their energies on getting the job done. In fact, some of the most enthusiastic people in the history of the world have been quiet, often withdrawn, and sometimes even shy.

The dictionary defines enthusiasm as a "warmth of feeling, a keen interest." It's a determination to keep your high and lofty promises to yourself and those you love.

It's Believing a Task Is Worth Doing!

The top salespeople in America will tell you that believing what they are doing is worthwhile makes them more creative, more excited about life, and more at peace with themselves. For them it is closely tied to their feelings of self-esteem.

It's Believing You Can Do It!

Enthusiasm is what happens when we see a task that really captures our imagination and something deep within us says, "I can do it."

When it happens, you become a dynamo of power. Mountains melt away before you, problems only redouble your efforts, and skeptics only kindle your determination. You discover you have inner resources you didn't know existed—in short, that you can do things you dared not try before.

Ray Kroc's epic achievements were slow to develop. At the age of 52, he set out with little more than an idea he believed worthwhile and a quiet, inner confidence that he could do it. His goal was to build a chain of hamburger restaurants—before there were any such things.

Twenty-two years later, his MacDonald's restaurants were all over the world and annual sales had reached $1 billion.

Enthusiasm is like the burst of energy a marathon runner feels after crashing through a "wall" of resistance. It's like the promise of the tiny light at the end of a long tunnel beckoning us on.

II. HOW DO YOU GET AND KEEP ENTHUSIASM?

Getting enthusiasm is a little like learning to breathe: Nobody can tell you exactly how to do it, but without it you're in big trouble. No one but you can discover that compelling purpose or exciting goal that ignites enthusiasm inside you, but you can learn a great deal from others about how to use it to maximum advantage.

Here are some insights I've learned from some real experts on enthusiasm; what's more, I've tested and proven them in the laboratory of my own life.

1. *Enthusiasm is born on the inside*

In the daily grind of life you can lose touch with what really matters. There are so many routine decisions to make, so many challenges to be met, and so many burdens to carry, that you can lose your perspective. However, as you connect with the enthusiasm planted deep within you, you'll feel it begin to grow and grow. Soon, you'll be back on track.

It's not the first mile of a long and arduous journey that gets to you—you're excited about getting started. And it's not the last mile— you're thrilled about getting there. The miles that get to you are the long and tedious ones in the middle where you can't see where you're coming from or where you're going.

Always remember that enthusiasm comes from the inside out, not vice versa. It's easier to motivate yourself from within than to pump yourself up with empty sayings.

2. *Enthusiasm grows when you focus on solutions and opportunities, not problems and circumstances*

Life for you will always be as you choose to see it. You can focus your attention on the problems and circumstances which surround you, or you can keep your eyes on the solutions and opportunities.

I recently read a story that illustrates it better than I can explain it. It seems that a number of farmers in Pennsylvania were sitting around complaining about the increasing cost of electricity and the unpleasant task of disposing of all the waste their cows generated. But the Waybright brothers and their brother-in-law, who run the Mason Dixon Farms near Gettysburg, decided to quit complaining about all the manure the cows were generating, and to do some generating of their own—electricity, that is. They built a power generator that runs on methane gas produced from heated manure from their 2,000 cows. Generating much of their own power, they cut their annual electricity bill from $30,000 to $15,000.

As you might guess, most of the other farmers laughed at the project and called it "Waybright's folly" (and other even less flattering names). They were satisfied to see their problems and to seek out their Congressmen to complain about their miserable circumstances.

But no one's laughing anymore. In fact farmers, Congressmen, and agriculture ministers from around the world are beating a steady path to the Mason Dixon farms. Soon the Waybright brothers will be selling some of their excess power to their once jeering neighbors.

And that's no bull!

Okay, so you're not in the cow business, and your biggest problem is not electricity bills, but the principle works in any area of life. Enthusiasm—with all the good things that go with it—comes when you turn your eyes from the problem or circumstance and focus on the solution and opportunity.

3. *Enthusiasm thrives around positive people*

A lot of people say that enthusisasm is contagious. My experience would indicate that negativism and pessimism are far more contagious. It is always easier to believe the worst than to hope for the best—especially if you are struggling against overwhelming odds. It's even worse when you're tired, or have just suffered a severe setback.

Don't waste your creative energies on people who are always putting you and your ideas down. Seek out those positive and successful people who can give you a boost.

If you want to be enthusiastic and have the enthusiasm which produces success, *always spend your time with positive, enthusiastic, and successful people.*

4. *Enthusiasm recharges itself on momentum*

Jerry Reed's popular song of a few years ago said it very nicely: "When you're hot, you're hot!" Believe me, it's more than empty words.

Of course, William Shakespeare said it with more eloquence in these famous lines from *Julius Caesar*:

"There is a tide in the affairs of men,
Which, taken at the flood, leads on to fortune;
Omitted, all the voyage of their life
Is bound in shallows and miseries."

It's when you feel most enthusiastic that you need to throw yourself into life's biggest challenge. Celebrate your greatest victories by plunging into even greater challenges. Take full advantage of the momentum you gain with each hard-earned step.

Nothing feeds enthusiasm like success, and nothing can hold back enough enthusiasm.

A BACKWARD GLANCE

Enthusiasm starts from within you, feeds on a positive mental attitude, and works best around positive and enthusiastic people.

I hope that in this book I have convinced you that selling is an honorable profession—that it's a career worthy of your best efforts. And I hope I've given you some tools that will help you become as successful as you'd like to be.

The high impact selling system has worked well for me!

It's working well for thousands of others!

I believe it will work well for you!

Here's hoping you get all you want out of life!

Index

195